Mookie Betts: The Inspiring Story of One of Baseball's All-Star Right Fielders

An Unauthorized Biography

By: Clayton Geoffreys

Table of Contents

Foreword

Mookie Betts has done a lot since entering the MLB. At the time of this writing, he is a five-time All-Star, two-time World Series Champion, American League Most Valuable Player and four-time Silver Slugger Award recipient. Betts has been a staple and critical part to every team he has been part of, from his beginnings with the Boston Red Sox to his latest stint with the Los Angeles Dodgers. Thank you for purchasing *Mookie Betts: The Inspiring Story of One of Baseball's All-Star Right Fielders*. In this unauthorized biography, we will learn Mookie Betts' incredible life story and impact on the game of baseball. Hope you enjoy and if you do, please do not forget to leave a review!

Also, check out my website at claytongeoffreys.com to join my exclusive list where I let you know about my latest books. To thank you for your purchase, you can go to my site to download a free copy of *33 Life*

Lessons: Success Principles, Career Advice & Habits of Successful People. In the book, you'll learn from some of the greatest thought leaders of different industries on what it takes to become successful and how to live a great life.

Cheers,

Clayton Geoffreys

Visit me at www.claytongeoffreys.com

Introduction

February 10, 2020, was a cold, dreary day for fans of the Boston Red Sox as they lost one of the game's greatest players, a player that they had grown to love ever since his debut against the Yankees nearly six years ago. In that short span, they had witnessed the evolution of a star from a boy drafted out of Overton High School in 2011 to a young man who played with poise and grace under pressure, whose irreproachable desire to win had propelled one of the greatest Red Sox teams of recent memory to a dominant World Series win over the Dodgers just sixteen months ago. Now only in memory would the number 50 jersey glide through the field in right and dash around the bases in Boston, the Red Sox faithful left to suffer the seemingly unforgivable decision by team executives to jettison one of the game's best.

It was October 20th, 1988, an all too distant memory for the Dodgers, the last time they had hoisted the

Commissioner's Trophy. They were a franchise in search of that final piece to push them to a title. They had made the playoffs seven straight times, their high watermark culminating in an excruciating Game 7 loss to the Houston Astros in the 2017 Fall Classic. And now as the news broke that Mookie Betts, who was not yet born when the Dodgers had last won a title, was headed to Chavez Ravine in a trade that shook the baseball world. Could this be it? Was Mookie the last piece to the championship puzzle?

Fast-forward seven months and it is game six of the World Series, the Dodgers just one win away and nursing a two to one lead in the bottom of the eighth inning. Into the box steps Mookie Betts and on a zero and two count, he redirects a hanging slider, courtesy of the Rays' reliever Pete Fairbanks into the left center field bleachers, leaving Dodgers fans to wonder with equal parts glee and apprehension if this could finally be their moment.

The Dodgers would, of course, go on to win Game Six and thus the 2020 World Series, capping off what was one of the most, if not perhaps *the* most extraordinary baseball seasons of all time, considering the context of the COVID-19 pandemic. And for Mookie Betts, his second World Series ring in just his first year with the Dodgers would solidify his reputation as one of baseball's most prestigious players. He would also finish second that year in voting for the National League MVP, having already won the American League MVP as a member of the Red Sox. Betts was a key catalyst for the 2018 team, which would win an astounding 108 regular season games en route to winning the World Series against the Dodgers, coincidentally his future team. The 2018 season was also monumental for Mookie on an individual level as he became the first player in the history of the American League to win the World Series while also being decorated with the MVP, Gold Glove, and Silver Slugger awards—All this from someone who stood at just five foot nine inches tall, almost an anomaly in today's day and age where athletes are earmarked by professional scouts first and foremost on size. Perhaps that was a reason as to why he fell to the fifth round, 172nd overall back in Major League Baseball's 2011 First Year Player Draft. He would also fail to appear in Baseball America's top 200 list of prospects that year. So he was, initially at least, not highly regarded by most scouts. But that would change and very quickly. Mookie's meteoric ascension is an incredible story where phenomenal talent was propelled by extraordinary dedication and perseverance to produce one of baseball's most electrifying personalities.

Chapter 1: Childhood and Early Life

Markus Lynn "Mookie" Betts was born to parents Diana Collins and Willie Betts on October 7th, 1992 in the city of Nashville, Tennessee. He was an incredibly active youngster, always running when he had the chance, and preferably with some sort of sports ball in his hands. His mother Diana, who worked for the Tennessee Department of Transportation, was his first baseball coach and precipitated his lifelong pursuit at the age of five by signing him up for Little League in Nashville.

It was not always easy from the start, though. Mookie, who had no siblings, was small for his age, a "Little bitty kid with little legs," as his mom would later recall. Because of this, he was rejected three times from local Little Leagues. [i] The last rejection hurt him as Mookie began to think he might not be able to play, the coach insisting that he was looking for bigger children in order to field a competitive team. However, his mother would have none of that. She was a former standout high school softball player who knew that her son had a special talent and more importantly that every child should have the chance to participate. And so, naturally, she started a new team with the children who had been rejected, her son included. The team might not have performed well, but they did score a significant win against the last coach to reject him. During that game, Mookie's team was struggling to record an out as the first baseman was dropping throws. Mookie's mother instructed him that whenever the ball was hit his way, he would have to take it himself to the bag in order to record the out. The very next ball was hit to Mookie, who was playing shortstop. He scooped the ball up and raced all the way to first base, diving in order to just beat the runner. This prompted complaints from the other team saying that Mookie was not playing the game the way he was supposed to be. His mother ignored the complaints and instead praised her son for running hard to get the out. It was this encouragement that fostered Mookie's desire to play baseball. And while his nickname was inspired by his mother's appreciation of the play of Mookie Blaylock, a guard for the NBA's Atlanta Hawks, perhaps it was his initials of MLB that ignited his destiny to one day be acclaimed among Major League's Baseball's brightest stars.

Mookie's father, Willie Betts, was born in Louisiana in 1943, a period of time where the abhorrent coercion of racial segregation was still upheld by the Jim Crow laws of the Deep South. He moved to Kentucky at a very young age and would later serve in the Air Force during the Vietnam War, afterwards leading a career as a railroad mechanic superintendent. He grew up with four brothers and two sisters who were told to never go easy on the younger children, and that they should have to always earn what they had. It was an early lesson that Mookie picked up when he first began playing ping-pong with his uncles, who would routinely beat him in the beginning, and sparked a competitive fire in him at a young age. [ii]

Mookie's parents separated when he was ten years old, but both maintained vital roles in raising him during his formative years. Mookie spent the school year with his mother in Brentwood, located in the suburbs of Nashville while his father, who was retired by that time, took him to his basketball and baseball practices during the summer. Both parents were a constant presence in the local sports community during his time in Overton High School, Mookie's teammates would affectionately refer to his father as 'Papa Willie' as he would be known to blow on a train whistle during key moments in the game while his mom attended the concession stand. [iii]

Mookie was all over the sports scene when he was young, and not just in baseball. His mother, an avid bowler with three hundred games to her credit, encouraged him to bowl at an early age. He played football until he was fourteen, and also a year of soccer. He played table tennis as well and became known for beating adults. He had an early predilection for basketball, and at one point he thought it might have been his choice sport, until, of course, his baseball talents took center stage.

When Mookie was ten, his father took him to visit a youth baseball camp at the University of Tennessee. During batting practice there, Mookie was thrown a difficult pitch to hit that was near the dirt, but like it was nothing, he adjusted his hands and swung, hitting a line drive into the field, displaying his incredible hand-eye coordination. This caught the attention of the volunteer head coach Rod Delmonico, who asked for the same sort of pitch again. The same result ensued and Delmonico was impressed. Before Mookie left, Delmonico addressed his father, telling him, "Your son needs to play baseball." [iv]

A traumatic, life-changing event would occur when Mookie was just twelve years old, something that altered his outlook on the value of life. In the Spring of 2005, Betts was asleep in the family SUV as they traveled to Kansas City, Missouri for a bowling tournament. The car, which was driven by his stepfather, struck a pole and rolled out onto the median, ejecting Betts in the process. Fortunately, though no one in the car was killed, his stepfather was airlifted to a hospital where he later recovered, while his mom suffered a broken shoulder. Betts himself sustained multiple injuries including a dislocated wrist and a swollen jaw. He spent about a week recovering in the hospital and was placed on a liquid diet. Later he dealt with the effects of post-traumatic stress disorder. He was, however, determined to go back to school and play baseball again as he could not bear the anguish of watching his teammates from a distance. A testament to his resolve even at a young age, he would eventually return to the field that year, somehow managing to hit with a cast on his right wrist. Reflecting on the event years later he would say, "You can't take anything for granted. At that point, I was like, life can be taken from you at any time". [v]

One of the things that precipitated Mookie's quick rise to the majors was his precocious ability to learn from mistakes as the fact that one should only make the same mistake once was something that his parents impressed upon him early. His father emphasized the importance of thinking about every action, not just how to do something, but why, as a means of being prepared for any situation. Having this sort of persistent mentality at an early age helped to nourish what would become perhaps Mookie's greatest attribute as a player: an astonishingly acute baseball acumen. "Always work hard. Be humble, because nothing is promised to you," was something his mother would always impress upon him. [vi] Mookie's extraordinary physical talent cannot be overstated, but there is little doubt that the virtues his parents instilled in him at a young age were ultimately paramount to his success.

Terry Shumpert, his mother's cousin, was a big leaguer who had had an extensive career spanning fourteen seasons with six different pro teams, most notably the Kansas City Royals and Colorado Rockies. Prior to the 2004 season, Shumpert, then thirty-seven, decided that it would be his last go-round. He would play out his final season for the Nashville Sounds, the Pittsburgh Pirates' Triple-A Minor League affiliate. That summer, Mookie's immersion into the baseball world would continue in earnest when he would regularly visit the ballpark in Nashville, scoring an opportunity to practice with the team. Three summers later in 2007, just before starting high school, Mookie would visit Shumpert again, this time in Colorado. Shumpert arranged a homerun hitting contest between Mookie and his son, Nick, who would later go on to be selected by the Detroit Tigers in the 2015 MLB draft. Mookie put on an impressive display, hitting several of the balls out of the yard. It was then that Shumpert saw the potential for greatness in his young cousin.

Mookie was eager to learn from Shumpert and they developed a mentor type of relationship. The dynamic between the two reminded the former big leaguer of his playing days with the legendary Hall of Famer Tony Gwynn. Back then, Shumpert would ask Gwynn the sort of questions that Mookie was asking him now. In a sort of passing of the torch type of moment, Shumpert shared what he learned from Gwynn with Mookie. [vii]

Chapter 2: High School Career

When Mookie entered Overton High School in the Fall of 2007, his reputation as a precocious sort of talent preceded him. Head coach Mike Morrison, who had been Overton's baseball coach for nearly a decade already, was acutely aware of Mookie's exploits on the field before he even had the chance to coach him. Early on, he was displaying the dynamic sort of skill set that would make him one of baseball's best. He was a force to be reckoned with on the field, a constant threat to the defense with not only his ability to slash line drives and draw walks, but with his speed too. It would soon become clear that Mookie was simply in a tier of his own. Years later, Morrison, who is still the coach at Overton to this day, would recount that he was undoubtedly the most athletic player he had ever coached. [viii]

Mookie was a standout on the basketball court as well. As the team's starting point guard, he averaged 14.4

points, 5.8 assists, 2.4 steals, and 2.9 rebounds during his senior year while earning the Most Valuable Player award in his district. Chris Hight, one of Mookie's basketball coaches, praised him not just for his athleticism, but for his knowledge of the game. He could dunk, yes, but he was also a proficient passer that was known to set up his teammates with high percentage looks. His athleticism was matched only by his astuteness, and he could always find the right play. His former coach believed that Mookie could have been one of the country's top collegiate point guards, had he chosen that path. [ix]

Mookie also bowled during the basketball season, due to his mother having taken him to the lanes before he even started school. He quickly became a force there as well. In 2010 a 221.4 average led to him earning the Tennessean Bowler of the Year award while leading the Bobcats to a 16-3 record and an appearance in the state quarterfinals. [x]And although he did not play on the gridiron in high school, his mother insisting that he stay out due to injury concerns, there existed plenty of tales from friends and coaches alike recounting his ability to fling the football as well as anyone. Even though he did not play, he wanted to participate with friends on the football team and he did that as the waterboy. When he was not with a team, the eclectic Betts was dominating the ping pong table and breezing through Rubik's cubes. His talent took center stage wherever he went including the classroom where he was an honors student who maintained a 3.5 GPA while enrolled in Advanced Placement courses. [xi]

After hitting for a sublime .549 batting average during his junior year, one professional scout quickly became enthralled by Mookie's burgeoning talent. Danny Watkins was a scout for the Boston Red Sox and had been since 2004, trailing Tennessee, Mississippi, Alabama, as well as portions of Florida. In June of 2010, he found himself at an annual high school baseball showcase at Middle Tennessee University located in Murfreesboro. His eyes were drawn to a flashy 17-year-old senior who made a scintillating play at shortstop. Watkins followed Mookie closely, observing with admiration the ease with which he played. He'd introduce himself to Mookie later that evening and would go on to follow him at a few other stops that summer. For Watkins it would soon become clear that the teenager from Tennessee was a legitimate talent and one that the Red Sox should highly covet in the upcoming 2011 draft. During the following fall, Watkins arranged for a meeting at a nearby restaurant with Mookie and his mother. He would try to convince him to go pro in lieu of college and sign with the Red Sox should they select him in the upcoming draft next June. [xii]

By that time, colleges had already begun recruiting him in earnest, the top two programs in the mix being Tennessee and Vanderbilt. Mookie, though, had reservations in attending Vanderbilt as he did not know if he would be a starter for their team right away. Vanderbilt's head coach Tim Corbin spoke to Overton high school coach Mike Morrison and expressed that he was taken aback when Mookie had told him that he was not sure if he was able to compete at that level yet. Morrison attributed the remark to Mookie's temperament stating that, "He was self-confident, but never over-confident." [xiii] He eventually chose the Volunteers, signing a letter of intent to attend the University of Tennessee. [xiv]

In his senior year, Mookie continued to dazzle with a .509 batting average while stealing 31 bases, his performance earning him an honorable mention on the Louisville Slugger High School All-American list. [xv]H eading into the June 2011 Draft, however, Mookie was not highly regarded. Many scouts were caught up by his lack of size which put into question his ability to hit for power.

There were, however, some scouts who were thoroughly convinced of his enormous potential. The Red Sox's Danny Watkins was one; another was Mark

Conner, who at the time was a second-year area scout operating out of Nashville for the San Diego Padres. Conner had first spotted Betts at a showcase in Lakeland Florida in 2010. He was struck not only by his athleticism and electric bat speed, but by the extraordinary poise with which he played. There seemed to be an air of tranquility to his game, a calmness in his demeanor that was uncommon for a seventeen-year-old. Conner observed that sort of unflappable personality watching Betts play basketball too. Betts participated in a private workout for Conner, his supervisor Sean Campbell, and the Padres' scouting director Jaron Madison which generated positive impressions. It quickly became clear that Conner, who had been awarded the Padres' 2010 Scout of the Year award, was on to something and that securing the under-the-radar shortstop from Tennessee should be a priority in the upcoming draft. [xvi]

Danny Watkins' initial glowing reports had caused Red Sox amateur scouting director Amiel Sawdaye to become enamored with the talented teen from Tennessee who had the sort of quick, explosive swing that drew comparisons to a former MVP in Andrew McCutchen. For Boston, Mookie had checked all the boxes. He was not only athletic but had extraordinary baseball acumen both on the bases and in the field. Defensively, he was not polished quite yet but he had the sort of speed to compensate and had already demonstrated that he was an extraordinarily quick learner. His work ethic was through the roof; his parents had seen to that. He had yet to build up his true power, but otherwise, his ability with the bat was superlative. His knowledge of the strike zone was advanced and his pitch recognition was there too. Very rarely did anyone see him fooled by an off-speed pitch. And then there were his hands: lightning-quick through the strike zone that allowed him to use the barrel of the bat to slash line drives to all fields. He was the antithesis of a one-dimensional pull-hitter. Simply put, he was a dynamic talent that was capable of tilting the outcome of a game at all levels, on the bases, in the field, and with his bat. [xvii]

Boston would win the race to call his name in the draft at pick 172, much to the disappointment of Mark Conner and the Padres who had the following pick. The 2011 draft would become a sort of case study in player evaluation, as it would go on to be regarded as one of the most loaded classes in recent memory featuring several players of star quality, including Anthony Rendon, Gerrit Cole, Francisco Lindor, and Javier Báez among others. [xviii] In the case of Betts, it turned out that he was clearly undervalued. Even Watkins himself had pegged Betts more so as a sixth-rounder. [xix] So Boston's decision to select him in the fifth round was, from what they knew at the time at least, a sort of calculated risk. That apparent risk, however, would turn out to be one of the most brilliant moves in the history of their franchise.

On draft day Mookie was playing video games in the basement of his mom's house with one of his high school teammates. A phone call forced him to pause. It was his agent. He'd been called by the Red Sox in the fifth round, 172nd overall. He went upstairs to talk to his mom. [xx]The ensuing decision would be easily the biggest of his life to that point. Would he sign with Boston in lieu of his commitment to attend the University of Tennessee and play for the Volunteers? For the Boston Red Sox, the question became financial negotiations. An interesting development occurred just prior to the draft when Todd Raleigh, the University of Tennessee's head baseball coach who had helped to secure Mookie's letter of intent, was fired, adding some uncertainty to his commitment to play there. Mookie himself was thoroughly undecided after the Red Sox drafted him, telling the Knoxville News Sentinel in an interview that even though Raleigh was gone he still was not opposed to attending UT; he just had to figure out what he actually wanted to do. [xxi]Bost on's eighth-round selection that year in Senquez Golson did not sign, freeing up some capital for negotiations. Mookie's parents, meanwhile, were insistent on a favorable signing bonus, their son's financial flexibility being paramount in the case that things did not work out. In August, just before the signing deadline struck, Mookie signed with Boston for $750,000, roughly $600,000 above slot. [xxii]

Chapter 3: Mookie's Meteoric Rise Through the Minors

Mookie's stay in the minor leagues was brief but his initial transition to professional baseball was a challenging one. While his former high school friend and teammates prepared for life at college, Mookie's signing precipitated the necessity for maturity as he prepared to launch his professional career. It was difficult early on and he would rely on the support of his family and high school friends, most notably Andrew Montgomery whom he confided in regularly. He struggled to distinguish himself in his first posting with the Short-Season A Spinners located in Lowell, Massachusetts, a long way from home. This was a legitimately challenging point in his journey. Reflecting on it later in an interview with *GQ* he said, "That was the first time in my life, really, that I failed miserably." His doubts even prompted him to enroll to take the ACT college admissions exam. He was on the verge of quitting baseball when he had a breakthrough. He tinkered with his swing mechanics, opting to ditch a leg kick that he had been accustomed to and he started to hit. [xxiii]

Beginning the 2013 season, he was promoted to Single-A Greenville located in South Carolina, just a few hours from home. Initially, the results were not there as he carried a rough-looking .157 batting average into May. He started to have some doubts and expressed to his cousin Terry Shumpert the fear of being potentially demoted. Shumpert laughed it off and assured Mookie that he was not going anywhere. The exchange sparked Betts' determination to continue his journey, and shortly afterward he spoke to his father and said, "I'm not gonna stay right here." [xxiv]There re was truth in those words.

Seeing friends and family at his games in Greenville made a world of difference and now with a year of experience under his belt, Mookie began to soar and never looked back. In Greenville he ended up hitting for a .296 batting average along with an excellent .418 OBP earning him distinction as a South Atlantic League All-Star. He led the league in walks and began to show some power too, knocking out eight home runs after none in the previous season at Lowell. On July 9th, he was promoted once again to High-A Salem. [xxv]Once there, he continued his assault on the minor leagues hitting for a .341 batting average and .414 on-base percentage, both stellar marks, along with eight home runs. He would finish the season on a high note, earning the 2013 Red Sox Minor League offensive player of the year award. [xxvi]

Mookie started the 2014 season with the Double-A Portland Sea Dogs, an aggressive assignment by the Red Sox considering that he was the tenth-youngest player in the Eastern League on Opening Day. It was a sign that the Red Sox had clear conviction in Mookie's precocious talent. He would reward their faith in him, as that season, he tied a minor-league record, getting on base in 71 consecutive games going back to the previous year and including postseason play. The record had been previously held by former Red Sox Kevin Youkilis and Kevin Millar. After 54 games into the season and while pacing the Eastern League with a .355 batting average, he was promoted to the final stop of the minor leagues, Triple-A Pawtucket where he was the second-youngest player in the league, trailing only the Cubs' Javier Báez. He played 23 games for the PawSox and began to make the challenging transition from second base to Center field, in anticipation of the Major Leagues where the former MVP Dustin Pedroia would block him from his natural position at the keystone. Across both Double-A and Triple-A that year he put together an impressive .345 batting average and .437 on-base percentage. [xxvii]It was clear that Mookie had nothing left to prove in the minor leagues. He was ready. Following a game in late June, Mookie was getting pizza with his then-girlfriend Brianna Hammonds, when he got a call from PawSox manager Kevin Boles who told him to come back to the field right away. He was perplexed as he headed back to the stadium that evening and he began to think that he may have done something wrong. Boles told him that the big-league club needed help, they had just released Grady Sizemore earlier that month and they needed an outfielder. He was getting the call up.

Chapter 4: The Precocious One

His parents received the news and along with Brianna, they flew right away to New York, their excitement palpable. But Mookie's reaction was subdued, almost blasé at first. He described it later on, saying, "It seemed like everyone else was a lot more excited than I was. I don't know if it was because I was nervous or something. That night I didn't get a whole lot of sleep." [xxviii] Slowly, though, the reality began to set in. That in the morning he would be going to New York to play against the New York Yankees at Yankee Stadium on Sunday Night baseball. More importantly, he had to go shopping in the morning because he needed a new suit.

After winning the 2013 World Series over the St. Louis Cardinals, expectations were high in Boston the following year. That offseason, however, they had lost a key player to free agency in outfielder Jacoby Ellsbury as he signed a seven-year pact with the division-rival Yankees. Prior to the season, Boston signed Grady Sizemore, who had not played since 2011 due to various injuries, to a one-year, incentive-laden deal. Boston's other two Opening Day outfielders were Mike Carp, who would make his final major-league appearance that season and Daniel Nava, who at thirty-one had yet to distinguish himself as anything more than a backup type of player. The Red Sox also had an aging veteran in Shane Victorino who was dealing with a back injury that kept him out through the first month of the season. It was a makeshift group of outfielders at best and it was only a matter of time before a certain star-to-be would have his chance.

Enter Mookie, who on June 29th, 2014 was set to make his Major League debut for a Boston team that badly needed a jolt of energy as they entered that Sunday night with a record of 37-44 seven games back in the division. The bright lights of Yankee Stadium and a huge crowd on hand set the stage for the future star who was starting in right field and hitting eighth. In his first at-bat facing the Yankee's starter Chase Whitley, he grounded into an inning-ending double-play. The Red Sox David Ortiz hit a three-run home run in the third inning to stake Boston to a four-to-nothing lead. Mookie had his second chance the following inning. He watched the first pitch, a slider, hit the outside part of the plate for a strike. The next pitch was a fastball up and out over the plate, Mookie did not hesitate this time, smacking it up the middle for a ground ball single. His mom, dad, and fiancée smiled and cheered from the stands as they watched him glide to first base. He was later caught trying to steal second base, tagged out by the future Hall-of-Famer Yankee Shortstop Derek Jeter. He drew a walk in his next plate appearance and scored the first run of his major-league career on a sacrifice fly off the bat of Dustin Pedroia. The Red Sox would go on to win that game by a score of 8-5. [xxix]

Three games later the Red Sox were back home in Fenway Park taking on the Chicago Cubs. In the bottom half of the fifth inning Mookie stepped up to the plate with a runner on and the Red Sox trailing 8-3. On a 2-1 count Mookie turned on and crushed a high and tight fastball from Cubs' reliever, Carlos Villanueva, sending the ball soaring high over the green monster, for his first career home run. [xxx] He was later sent back down to the minor leagues twice that summer, once to make room on the active roster for Shane Victorino, who was returning from an injury. Regardless, it was merely bookkeeping as the Red Sox shuffled their roster. Mookie's place was in the Major League, and he stayed there for the rest of the year following another call up on August 18th. [xxxi]

He quickly became a star, one that the fans began to adore. But Mookie was modest, or perhaps even oblivious to the attention he was receiving. During his second call up to the majors, Mookie, Brianna, and his close friend from high-school Andrew Montgomery were getting food at a local establishment, when Montgomery pointed out that he saw a fan coming out who had a stunned expression on his face upon seeing Betts. The fan was too bashful to introduce himself, and Mookie did not realize it. He did not believe it either when his friend pointed it out to him. Early on, Mookie clung to a tight group of family and friends for support, including his parents, his girlfriend Brianna, close friends from high school, and his cousin Terry Shumpert. [xxxii]

The Red Sox, meanwhile, continued their descent in the standings. At the trade deadline was in late July, the team had to make the difficult decision to trade away the veteran Jon Lester, who had spent his entire career in Boston and had won two World Series with them back in 2007 and in 2013. On August 29th, the Red Sox's record stood at a dismal 58-75 as they began a three-game set to take on the division rival Rays at Tampa Bay. The Rays starting pitcher Chris Archer ran into trouble in the top half of the second inning, allowing a double to Yoenis Cespedes before issuing a walk to Mike Napoli and plunking Daniel Nava. The bases were loaded for Mookie, who proceeded to unload on a 1-0 pitch, sending a line drive to the bleachers in left, his first career grand slam. And in doing so, Mookie, at age twenty-one, became the youngest Red Sox to hit a grand slam since Tony Conigliaro back in 1965. Mookie had not been in the majors long, but he had already impressed Red Sox manager John Farrell with his incredible bat speed, which allowed him to tap into more power than his modest five-foot-nine frame had suggested. [xxxiii]

The Red Sox would later lose second-baseman Dustin Pedroia to a wrist injury which allowed them to send Mookie back to his natural position. Boston still viewed him as a future outfielder, but in the meantime, he would finish out the season defensively in the infield.[xxxiv] The 2014 season came to a close with Boston finishing in last place in the division with a final record of 71-91. In an interesting note, Boston became the first team in baseball history to come in last place, win the world series, then come in last place again in a three-year stretch.[xxxv] Mookie eventually received a promotion to the leadoff spot in the lineup and finished the season with a .291 batting average, .368 on-base percentage, and seven stolen bases across 213 plate appearances. [xxxvi] These were impressive totals, but merely hinting at the greatness yet to come.

Excitement was renewed heading into the 2015 season. Not only had Mookie shown enough the prior year to be excited about as a potential player to build around, but the Red Sox had made two significant free agent signings. The first was a five-year deal with the third-baseman Pablo Sandoval, who had helped the San Francisco Giants win three World Series. The second was outfielder Hanley Ramirez, a three-time all-star who came up originally as a Red Sox team member before being traded back in 2005, who Boston secured with a four-year deal worth $88 million. [xxxvii]

Opening Day, April 6th, Mookie was hitting leadoff and playing in center as Boston was taking on the Philadelphia Phillies. In the top of the third inning, facing the Phillies' ace lefty Cole Hamels, Mookie drilled a fly-ball home run to left field. That home run at just 22-years-old made him the third-youngest player to hit a home run on opening day in the history of the franchise, the youngest being Tony Conigliaro at the age of 20 in 1965. Boston took the opener by a score of 8-0. xxxviii A week later, April 13th, was the Red Sox's home opener at Fenway Park. Mookie electrified the Fenway faithful in the top of the first inning when he leaped high over the right-center field fence to rob the Washington Nationals' Bryce Harper of a home run. In the bottom of the first inning, Mookie got on base with a leadoff walk. With David Ortiz at the plate, he proceeded to steal second. As he slid into second base, he astutely realized that no one was covering third base with the defense in the shift for the left-handed-hitting Ortiz and quickly popped up and dashed to third, stealing two bases on the same play. Ortiz would later drive him in on a single. He was not done yet. In his next at-bat he drove a pitch off Nationals' starter Jordan Zimmermann into the left-field seats for a three-run home run. The Red Sox would go on to win their home opener, nine to four, thanks to Mookie who demonstrated his dynamic ability to affect the game not only as a hitter, but in the field, and on the basepaths too. [xxxix]

It was not all perfect for the rookie, though. He made some mistakes of the proverbial rookie kind, including getting caught stealing third with his team down just a single run. Mookie was tough on himself at times, but his veteran teammate Shane Victorino proved to be a valuable mentor, helping him get past the mistakes and learn from them. On June 12th, Mookie crashed into the center field wall and would miss the next couple of games with a minor leg injury. During that time off, Mookie, who was struggling at that point hitting just .237, sought after the advice of teammates Dustin

Pedroia and David Ortiz who were also two of the game's best hitters. [xl] Something clicked, because in the following week Mookie proceeded to pace the American League in hits, batting average, total bases, and on-base percentage. His performance earned him American League player of the week honors. [xli]

Mookie's surge, however, could not help Boston from yet again sliding in the standings. By the end of July, they had fallen to a record of 46-58, and were thoroughly out of the playoff race, fourteen games back in the loss column from the division-leading New York Yankees. [xlii] In August, there came unfortunate news as Boston manager John Farrell announced that he was diagnosed with lymphoma and would step down for the remainder of the season. Bench coach Torey Lovullo replaced him as interim manager, [xliii] and the Red Sox would end up finishing the regular season in last place for the second year in a row with a final record of 78-84. New acquisitions Hanley Ramirez and Pablo Sandoval were both massive disappointments, each finishing the season with an on-base percentage under .300, career-lows up until that point for both players. For Mookie, his first full season in the Major Leagues was a productive one as he hit for a .291 batting average and .341 on-base percentage while leading the team in both runs scored with 92 and stolen bases with 21. [xliv]

Chapter 5: The 2016 and 2017 Seasons & a Star on the Horizon.

The 2016 season would end up being a season of growth for both the Red Sox and Mookie Betts. Early in the offseason, it was announced that John Farrell would return as manager after undergoing successful treatment for lymphoma. [xlv] The Red Sox would also make a significant move in their front office announcing the hiring of Dave Dombrowski as President of Baseball Operations while the former General Manager, Ben Cherington, was stepping down. [xlvi]Dombrowski was aggressive as he tried to get Boston back to a winning record after two lost seasons. He addressed the bullpen, which had been an area of weakness, by acquiring Craig Kimbrel, regarded as one of the game's best closers, from the San Diego Padres in exchange for four prospects. [xlvii] A few weeks later Dombrowski made another move, signing free agent starting pitcher David Price to a seven-year deal worth $217 million. At the time it was the largest ever given to a pitcher. One of the areas of weakness for the Red Sox had been their rotation, as they did not have an ace. Price fit the bill as he led the American League with a 2.45 ERA in 2015 while also finishing second in voting for the American League Cy Young. [xlviii]

On May 31st, the Red Sox were at Camden Yards taking on the Baltimore Orioles. Mookie led off the game with a bang, redirecting a 1-0 fastball from starter Kevin Gausman, and depositing it past the 410 sign in Center field. In his next at-bat in the top of the second with two outs and two runners on, he victimized Gausman yet again tucking his hands in and yanking a high and inside fastball, a screeching line drive that just cleared the foul pole in left to give Boston a 5-2 lead. In the top of the seventh inning, he continued his assault on Orioles pitching, this time driving an outside fastball courtesy of reliever Dylan Bundy the opposite way over the right field fence. [xlix] It was his first three home run performances of his career and there would be more to come. Meanwhile, the Red Sox had gotten off to a strong start and by the end of May, they had a three-game lead in the division with a record of 32-20. [1]

Mookie continued to dazzle in the first half of the year and in just his second full season he was announced as a starter in the All-Star Game, along with three of his teammates: Xander Bogaerts, Jackie Bradley Jr, and David Ortiz. [li] He continued his scintillating play in July hitting for a .368 batting average that month along with a .415 on-base percentage while pacing the league in doubles earning him AL player of the month honors. By the end of July, he had already hit 22 home runs after hitting 18 in all of 2015. [lii]Boston's young star outfielder was reaching new heights. On August 14th, he sent the fans at Fenway into a frenzy as recorded his second three home run performance, two of them coming off of Zack Greinke, who was one of the National League's best pitchers and an All-Star that year. He finished the night with a whopping eight

RBIs. With his second three home run performance of the season, Mookie joined a select group, only twenty other players in baseball history had done it and the only other Red Sox to do so was none other than the immortal legend Ted Williams. [liii]

The Red Sox, meanwhile, continued to flourish, finishing the season on a high note with an eleven-game winning streak during September. After two losing seasons, the Red Sox finished with a 93-67 record and won the division with a convincing five-game lead. [liv]Offensively, the Red Sox were a juggernaut leading the league in runs scored at 878, in team batting average at .282, and in on-base percentage at .348. [lv]They were led by Boston legend David Ortiz, who had announced that 2016 would be his final season. And what a year it was, the three-time World Series champion and soon-to-be forty-one-year-old, finished the season pacing the league in doubles, RBI, and slugging percentage. His 38 home runs and 127 RBI were the most ever in a final season. [lvi]

Mookie was the engine at the top of the Red Sox lineup as he led the team in runs scored with 122, hits with 214, and stolen bases with 26, while also establishing new career-highs in home runs with 31 and batting average at .318. [lvii]He was the first player in baseball that season to reach 200 hits, doing so on September 20th. Up to that point, Mookie was also just the seventh player in baseball history to record 200 hits, 30 home runs, 40 doubles, and 20 stolen bases in the same season. And only one other player had done that at age 23 or younger: former Red Sox shortstop Nomar Garciaparra who did it in his rookie season of 1997. Mookie was in good company. Ortiz offered nothing but praise for the young star and his unrelenting work ethic, "It's unbelievable, he works so hard every day. Like I say, man, these kids, they're not playing around. They are up to the challenge." [lviii]

Their next challenge would be facing the Cleveland Indians in the American League Divisional Series. In Game 1 Red Sox starter Rick Porcello, who won the

American League Cy Young Award that year, was not up to the task as he allowed three home runs in the bottom half of the third inning. Boston would come close with Brock Holt hitting a home run in the top of the eighth to make it just a 5-4 deficit but that would end up being the final score. [lix]

In Game 2, 2014 Cy Young Award winner Corey Kluber was brilliant shutting out the Red Sox across seven frames. Meanwhile, David Price struggled for Boston, as he was tagged for five runs across just three and one-third innings of work. Mookie had one of the Red Sox three hits that night, a single in the top of the sixth as their offense was shut out, and the Indians took Game 2 in dominant fashion by a final score of 6-0. [lx]After dropping the second game, Boston found itself facing elimination in the best of five series.

Game 3 was another close contest. Mookie hit a double in the bottom of the sixth and would score a run in the bottom of the eighth off a Hanley Ramirez single. But in the end, it was not enough as Boston dropped game 3 by a final of 4-3 and was swept out the door, their postseason dreams dashed. [lxi]The Indians would go on to the World Series where they would ultimately lose to the Cubs in a seven-game affair that would feature one of the most dramatic finishes of recent memory. Although it ended in disappointment for the Red Sox, 2016 was a tremendous season for Mookie individually as he not only earned American League MVP consideration, finishing second in voting to Mike Trout, [lxii]but also took home his first Gold Glove award in recognition of his defensive ability. [lxiii]

Heading into the 2017 season, the Red Sox had established a promising young core of position players, led, of course, by Mookie, along with shortstop Xander Bogaerts, centerfielder Jackie Bradley Jr, and left fielder Andrew Benintendi, who had made his Major League debut last August. Hopes were heightened when the Red Sox pulled the trigger on one of the most notable trades in recent memory, sending high-profile prospects in Yoán Moncada and Michael Kopech to the Chicago White Sox in exchange for the left-hander Chris Sale, who was widely regarded as one of the best starting pitchers in baseball, who had at that point recorded a sensational career ERA of 3.00 across well over 1,000 innings pitched. [lxiv] Chris Sale and David Price now gave the Red Sox two dominant starters at the top of their rotation.

Similar to 2016, the Red Sox started off strong, finishing June with a record of 45-35 and a one-game lead in the division. [lxv] On Sunday afternoon, July 2nd, the Red Sox were finishing a three-game set at Toronto. Mookie's day got off to a less-than-ideal start as he struck out in the first inning. In the second inning, he hit a single to left field, scoring shortstop Tzu-Wei Lin. In the fourth inning, he stepped up to the plate with two runners on and deposited Blue Jays starter Joe Biagini's 2-0 offering into the center field stands for a three-run homerun, to give the Red Sox a five-to-one advantage. The rout was on but Mookie was not done. He would end up with two more hits including another home run finishing with eight RBIs which tied a major-league record for RBIs in a single game from a leadoff hitter. [lxvi]Later that month, he was selected to his second straight All-Star game, along with teammates Chris Sale and Craig Kimbrel. [lxvii]

The Red Sox finished the 2017 season with a 93-69 and once again won the division. Relative to 2016, 2017 was a down year for Mookie as he finished with a .264 batting average after the previous year's .318. Regardless, he still finished with a very respectable .344 on-base percentage while leading the team in runs scored, hits, RBI, home runs, and stolen bases. [lxviii]

The Red Sox then faced the Astros in the 2017 American League Divisional Series. Houston had the higher seed having ended the season with a 101-61 record and had home field advantage. Game 1 was a rout in favor of Houston as Red Sox ace Chris Sale struggled, allowing seven earned runs on nine hits in over five innings. Mookie had made two of the Red Sox eight hits as they dropped the series opener by a score of 8-2. [lxix]

Game 2 started off with the Astros ambushing Red Sox starter Drew Pomeranz for four early runs. The Red Sox offense was not able to muster up much of a fight; Mookie included who finished the night with just a double in his first-at-bat. Game 2 ended with the same score of 8-2. [lxx] Down 0-2 and facing elimination, the scene shifted to Fenway Park for Game 3. Through six innings, it was a tight contest with Boston holding the 4-3 advantage. The Red Sox offense broke the game open with a six-run outburst in the bottom of the seventh, the key hit coming off the bat of Hanley Ramirez, a two-run double to make it a 6-3 game. Mookie finished with another quiet night with just one hit along with three strikeouts. But the Red Sox had staved off elimination, taking Game 3 by a score of 10-3. [lxxi]

Unlike the first three, Game 4 was a nail-biter until the end. Xander Bogaerts hit a home run in the home half of the first to tie the score at 1-1. Mookie misplayed a liner from Yuli Gurriel allowing him to get a third, George Springer eventually knocked him in to push the Astros ahead 2-1. The Red Sox had a couple of chances to get back on the board but could not push anything across until Andrew Benintendi finally broke through with a two-run home run just past the pesky pole in right. The Red Sox now held a precarious 3-2 lead; the tension at Fenway was palpable, but the lead was gone in a blink when Alex Bregman sent a fly ball soaring way over the green monster in left to lead off the eighth inning. The Astros pushed across a couple of more runs to take a 5-3 lead heading into the bottom of the ninth. An exhilarating inside-the-park home run from Rafael Devers to the triangle in center put Boston within one run, but that would be all as the Astros took game 4 by a score of 5-4. [lxxii]

The 2017 Astros would go on to win the World Series, but it would be one that was later tainted by a sign-stealing scandal. Overall, it was a second quiet postseason appearance for Mookie, who finished with just two extra-base hits and no RBI. The Red Sox and Mookie had established a winning team; now it was time to prove that they were a championship team. Perhaps, the third time would indeed prove to be the charm.

Chapter 6: A Transcendent 2018 Season

In 2017, the Red Sox had taken a step back offensively, having lost David Ortiz, who had led the team in home runs and RBI in 2016, to retirement. They bolstered their lineup by signing outfielder J.D. Martinez to a five-year contract worth $110 million. [lxxiii] Martinez had become one of baseball's most prolific hitters and had finished third in home runs with 45 the previous season as a member of the Detroit Tigers and Arizona Diamondbacks in spite of playing in only 119 games. The team was also excited to see what third baseman Rafael Devers could do in his first full season. Devers was one of Boston's top-hitting prospects who had debuted last July following the team releasing Pablo Sandoval, who had ended up being a colossal disappointment. [lxxiv]The Red Sox had also dismissed manager John Farrell after last year's disappointing loss in the divisional round to the Astros and announced his successor, former Astros bench coach Alex Cora, during last year's postseason. [lxxv]

Following two quick exits in the postseason and now with a new manager and another expensive player under contract in J.D. Martinez, fans were restless and expectations were soaring in Boston heading into the 2018 season.

The Red Sox got off to a torrid start with a 12-2 record two weeks into the season. Mookie was sensational during that span, hitting for a .353 batting average along with a .452 on-base percentage. [lxxvi] On April 17th, the Red Sox were in Anaheim beginning a three-game set with the Angels. In the first inning, facing the Japanese star Shohei Ohtani, who would later take Rookie of the Year honors, Mookie pulled a 3-2 fastball deep past the left-centerfield wall. He went on to hit two more home runs that evening off relievers Luke Bard and Cam Bedrosian, making it his third three home run performance of his career. [lxxvii]

A little over two weeks later, Mookie continued to shock the baseball world with his exploits. On May

2nd, the Red Sox were at Fenway hosting the Royals. Leading off the bottom of the fourth inning, with Boston trailing 4-0, Mookie sent a 1-1 offering from Royals starter Danny Duffy deep past the green monster in left. In his next at-bat in the bottom half of the fifth, with the game tied 3-3, he took the Royals starter deep again. And then, much to the dismay of Danny Duffy, he hit another one, this time a mammoth blast to center field to stake Boston to a 5-3 lead. Mookie finished the day with a perfect four-for-four, raising his season average to a scintillating .365. [lxxviii] He reached his own historic milestone as his fourth game with three home runs broke the Red Sox record previously held by none other than Ted Williams, the greatest hitter who ever lived. [lxxix]

By the end of May the Red Sox had a record of 39-18 and were tied in the loss column with the division rival New York Yankees. [lxxx] As the calendar turned to June, Mookie suffered a minor injury, an abdominal strain, that required a brief ten-day stint on the injured list. On

July 6th, the Red Sox were on the road, facing the Kansas City Royals at Kauffman Stadium. Mookie led the game with a home run off Jason Hammel, the 100th of his career. He joined the special group of Tony Conigliaro, Jim Rice, and Ted Williams as the only hitters in Red Sox history to make such an achievement before their 26th birthday. [lxxxi]

On July 8th, baseball announced the rosters for the upcoming All-Star game in San Diego. Mookie was, of course, the starting right fielder for the American League. He was joined by teammates J.D. Martinez, Mitch Moreland, Chris Sale, and Craig Kimbrel. [lxxxii] As the calendar flipped to August, the Red Sox had established themselves as the class of the American League with a 75-34 record and a commanding five-game lead in the A.L. East. [lxxxiii] On August 9th, in a game against the Blue Jays in Toronto, Mookie hit a ninth inning home run off Ken Giles. The Red Sox would drop the contest 8-5, but it was a significant home run as he completed the cycle for the first time in his career having hit a single, double, and triple in his previous at-bats. He finished the night a perfect four-for-four, raising his batting average to .347, leading all hitters. [lxxxiv]

A few weeks later, with the regular season drawing to a close, Mookie stole his 30th base of the season in game one of a double-header against the Orioles at Fenway Park. It was not only a career-high but also put him in exclusive company, making him just the 40th player in the history of Major League Baseball to record 30 stolen bases and 30 home runs in the same season. He was also just the second Red Sox to accomplish this feat, the only other being Jacoby Ellsbuy back in 2011. In that same game, J.D. Martinez hit his 42nd home run of the year, which tied him with Dick Stuart for the most home runs by a player in their first season with the Boston Red Sox. Not just Mookie, but several players on the team were having sensational years, including shortstop Xander Bogaerts who had driven in a career-best 100 RBI.

Bogaerts acknowledged that the stars had seemingly aligned this season, saying, "We're having an amazing time this year. This is the best team I've been a part of, talent-wise and the coaching staff. It's just been amazing." [lxxxv]

The 2018 Red Sox would go on to win an astounding 108 games surpassing the franchise record of 105 back in 1912, the year Fenway Park was built. They were the first Red Sox team to surpass 100 wins since 1946. [lxxxvi] They also had the most regular season wins by a team since the 2001 Seattle Mariners, who won 116 games. Offensively, the team was a juggernaut, pacing all of baseball in not only runs scored (876) but in batting average (.268) and on-base percentage (.339) as well. [lxxxvii]

Mookie finished the season leading the Major League in batting average (.346) and slugging percentage (.640) while also tying Cleveland Shortstop Francisco Lindor with the most runs scored at 129. Mookie had also established career-highs in both home runs and stolen bases. [lxxxviii] In a day and age where strikeouts had become increasingly prevalent as a sacrifice for hitting home runs, Mookie was extraordinary in his ability to make contact, maintaining a near-even walk-to-strikeout rate while also hitting for power. In 2018 he undoubtedly grew as a hitter, becoming one of the game's most adept two-strike hitters while also learning how to drive pitches on the outer half of the plate for power. [lxxxix]He also received his third straight Gold Glove award in recognition of his defensive prowess. He tied for second among all outfielders with 20 defensive runs saved[xc] and was charged with only a single error, maintaining a .996 fielding percentage. [xci] He had transcended the game's upper echelon both offensively and defensively.

Capturing the American League's top seed, the Red Sox had secured their home field advantage and were set to renew their long-established rivalry with the New York Yankees in the American League Divisional Series. The Yankees were an upstart team, having surprised baseball last year by defeating the then-reigning World Series Champions, the Cleveland Indians in the ALDS before falling to the eventual World Series Champions, the Houston Astros in what turned out to be a tightly-contested, seven-game series. Hopes were high in the Bronx, having fallen just a game short of the World Series the year before. They had defeated the Oakland Athletics in the win-or-go-home Wild Card game and were now set to face Boston in the postseason for the first time since the infamous 2004 ALCS which saw the Red Sox mount a historic and stunning comeback after losing the first three games en route to winning their first Word Series title since 1918, in the process breaking the so-called curse of the Bambino. The 2018 season saw the American League produce three teams with 100 wins: the Yankees, Astros, and the Red Sox, a first in baseball history. [xcii]

The Yankees, having already used their best starting pitcher Luis Severino in the wild card game two nights earlier, turned to J.A. Happ to start Game 1. The Yankees had acquired the left-handed Happ from the Blue Jays just prior to the trade deadline that year and he had pitched well for them, carrying a 2.69 ERA through eleven starts. He quickly got into trouble, however, with J.D. Marinez hitting a three-run shot in the bottom half of the first. Mookie led off the bottom of the third inning with a double and would later score to make it a 4-0 Boston lead. The Yankees would threaten as Aaron Judge hit a home run off closer Craig Kimbrel in the ninth inning to close the gap to one run, but Boston finished the deal, taking Game 1 by a score of 5-4. [xciii]

Game 2 saw the Yankees bounce back as they chased Boston starting pitcher David Price early en route to a convincing 6-2 win to tie the series at one game each. The series shifted to the Bronx for Game 3. [xciv] As he had done so often that year, Mookie started things for Boston as he came around to score after leading off the third inning with a single off Yankee starter Luis

Severino. In the following inning, Mookie once again started the scoring, this time plating a run with a bases loaded walk. Boston went on a seven-run outburst that inning and proceeded to thoroughly embarrass and dismantle the Yankees in front of their home crowd, handing them a 16-1 [xcv] drubbing, significant as it was the worst playoff loss in Yankee franchise history. [xcvi]

The following night, Boston broke the run column first courtesy of J.D. Martinez and his sacrifice fly off Yankee starter C.C. Sabathia in the top of the third. Boston would score two more runs in the frame, taking an early 3-0 lead. Boston catcher Christian Vázquez led off the top of the fourth inning with a leadoff home run off Yankee reliever Zack Britton to make it 4-0. The Yankees would threaten in the bottom of the ninth, scoring two runs to make it a 4-3 contest, but Red Sox closer Craig Kimbrel stranded the tying run on second, retiring Gleyber Torres on a groundout to third to end it.[xcvii] Mookie had another quiet game at the plate with just a walk to go along with two strikeouts; regardless, his team got the job done handing their archrivals a crushing blow as they prepared to exact revenge on the Astros in the next round, the team who had ended their playoff hopes a year ago.

The American League Championship Series brought together two of baseball's juggernauts that year having combined for 211 wins. [xcviii] There was added intrigue in that Boston's new manager this year, Alex Cora, had been the Astros bench coach last season. The Astros were led by their emerging young star, third-baseman Alex Bregman. He had a breakout season not only establishing career-highs in home runs with 31, but also pacing the league in doubles with 51 along with an outstanding .394 on-base percentage. [xcix]

Game 1 featured two of baseball's most dominant starting pitchers in Houston's Justin Verlander, a former Cy-Young award winner, and Chris Sale who had been brilliant in his first two regular seasons in Boston with an ERA of 2.56 and a win-loss record of

29-12. [c] In the top half of the second inning, George Springer started the scoring with a bases loaded, single-plating shortstop Carlos Correa and catcher Martin Maldonado giving Houston an early 2-0 lead. Boston's ace Sale ended up uncharacteristically struggling with his control, issuing four walks and was chased after just four innings. His counterpart, however, was just a little bit better that night as Verlander managed to bottle up Boston's stout lineup, allowing just two runs through six innings. Boston ended up dropping the series opener by a score of 7-2, but like all championship teams they would prove to be a resilient group. [ci]

Mookie led off the bottom half of the first inning with a double off Astros' starter Gerrit Cole and would later score the game's first run. Houston, however, would come charging right back the next inning, George Springer tying the game up with a two-run double off Boston starter David Price. In the bottom of the third inning, Jackie Bradley Jr came up with a huge, two-out, bases-clearing double that swung the game in favor of Boston, 5-4. Mookie led off the seventh and got on base with a walk before scoring again giving Boston a two-run advantage. The Red Sox went on to take Game 2 by a final of 7-5, [cii] Mookie's two runs scored proved pivotal as the Red Sox avoided falling into the dreaded 0-2 hole.

For Game 3, the scene shifted to the Astros Minute Maid Park where Boston won a convincing 8-2 victory, the key hit being a grand slam courtesy of Jackie Bradley Jr. [ciii]In Game 4, Mookie once again scored the first run for Boston after being plunked by Astros' starter Charlie Morton. This game ended up being an entertaining and tightly contested back and forth affair that saw the Astros briefly take the lead in the bottom half of the fifth 5-4, before Boston took the lead back the following inning with a two-run home run by Jackie Bradley Jr. off Houston reliever Josh James. Mookie later hit a single in the top of the eighth and proved his mettle as a base runner advancing to second on a wild pitch before scoring on a single to center field from J.D. Martinez. Boston closer Craig Kimbrel made things tense in the bottom of the ninth, walking the bases loaded for Alex Bregman but the Astros' third baseman lined out to left, sealing the Red Sox victory by a final score of 8-6. [civ]

By Game 5, Red Sox fans were buzzing with anticipation as they had watched their team fall in Game 1, then reel off three straight wins, putting them just one win away from dethroning the reigning champs and punching their ticket to their first World Series appearance since 2013. David Price, Boston's starting pitcher, struck out Carlos Correa, stranding José Altuve at first base to end the first. Justin Verlander was on his game for the Astros as well and matched zeroes with Price through the first two innings. In the top half of the third, however, the Red Sox were the first to break the run column, J.D. Martinez sending a hanging breaking ball into the Crawford boxes in left field putting Boston ahead 1-0.

A pitcher's duel ensued. Both Price and Verlander continued to pitch well with no scoring in the fourth or fifth innings; then in the top of the sixth, Red Sox first baseman Mitch Moreland led off, clanging a ball off the left field wall for a double, with second baseman Ian Kinsler following with a single. Up was the lefty-swinging Rafael Devers and he delivered the knockout punch, taking a high and tight 98 mile-per-hour fastball the opposite way just over the fence in left. [cv] The Red Sox dugout erupted as he rounded the bases. Mookie was there to greet his teammate at the top step of the dugout with a big grin on his face as he congratulated him and took his batting helmet off. The rest of the game passed with few histrionics; Mookie and his Red Sox had won the American League Pennant. Now all that there was left to do was wait and see who won the National League Championship Series, as the Los Angeles Dodgers had beaten the Milwaukee Brewers the night before to tie the series at two games each.

Two nights later, the baseball world watched as the Dodgers ended up beating the Brewers in a dramatic Game 7, sending them to the World Series for the second year in a row. The Dodgers had been in the postseason every year since 2013 and had most recently fallen painfully short, losing last year's fall classic, a gut-wrenching seven-game series against the Astros. They had been aggressive at the trade deadline, acquiring Orioles' slugger Manny Machado and winning the National League West for the sixth straight season after defeating the Colorado Rockies in a tie-breaker game. [cvi]In the divisional round, the Dodgers defeated the Braves in four games prior to their battle with the Brewers for the N.L. pennant.

During Game 1 of the World Series, at Fenway Park, Red Sox ace Chris Sale retired Manny Machado to end the top half of the first inning, stranding David Freese at first base. In the bottom half of the first, Mookie made the Fenway faithful excited early as he led off with a hard single to center field off the Dodgers' storied ace Clayton Kershaw. He then proceeded to steal second base and scored the first run of the 2018 World Series courtesy off a Benintendi single to right. J.D. Martinez knocked in Benintendi with a single to left to give Boston an early 2-0 lead. The Dodgers rallied, tying it up with a Manny Machado single, scoring Justin Turner. The game was tied 3-3 when Mookie led off the bottom half of the fifth inning and did what he had done all year: get on base--this time working a walk off Kershaw. He advanced to third on a wild pitch and scored on a Xander Bogaerts groundout to second base, once again giving the Red Sox the lead. Boston scored again in the inning, an RBI single from Rafael Devers, taking a 5-3 lead into the sixth. In the bottom half of the seventh, Red Sox infielder Eduardo Nuñez blew up what was at the time a close 5-4 game with a three-run shot, producing the game's final score of 8-4. [cvii]

Game 2 featured two lefty starters in Boston's David Price and the Dodgers' Hyun-Jin Ryu. Once again,

Boston fired the opening salvo, scoring first, an RBI single from second baseman Ian Kinsler in the bottom of the second. The second game of the series was a close one, the score 2-1 in favor of the Dodgers heading into the bottom of the fifth. Boston then fired back, loading the bases for Steve Pearce who walked in a run. Mookie, who had reached base on a single, then scored the go-ahead and what would end up being the winning run on a two-out J.D. Martinez single. Game 2 came to an end with a final score of 4-2. [cviii]

With Boston in command two games to none, the series shifted two nights later to Los Angeles. Game 3 would turn out to be one of the most memorable contests in World Series history. The Dodgers were the first to score, lefty-swinging outfielder Joc Pederson sending a ball into the stands in right off starter Rick Porcello. And then both offenses fell silent. The Red Sox were unable to muster anything against the Dodger's Walker Buehler, the hard-throwing righty out of Vanderbilt, who would finish third in National

League rookie of the year voting that season. Heading into the eighth, Boston trailed 1-0 as they faced Dodgers' reliever Kenley Jansen whose cut fastball had recorded 268 regular season saves. The inning started innocently with two outs, a flyball from Brock Holt followed by a strikeout of Devers. Into the batter's box stepped Jackie Bradley Jr, who had two big home runs in the ALCS, then scored yet another big hit in his bat. On a 2-0 pitch, he turned on a 93 mile per hour cut fastball sending it into the seats in right. That timely flyball over the right field wall precipitated one of the greatest marathons in World Series history. In the bottom of the eighth inning, Red Sox reliever Matt Barnes kept the game tied. Jansen followed suit in his second inning of work, retiring the Red Sox in order in the top of the ninth. In the bottom of the ninth, Dodgers outfielder Cody Bellinger led off with a single off David Price before getting thrown out on a baserunning gaffe. Craig Kimbrel came in for the Red Sox and finished out the home half of the ninth. In the top of the tenth, Ian Kinsler pinch ran for J.D. Martinez who got on base with a one-out walk. He was later gunned down attempting to score on a fly ball off the bat of Rafael Devers. Through twelve innings, the game remained tied 1-1. Then in the top of the 13th, a breakthrough in the offensive malaise ensued, or rather a defensive miscue. Brock Holt led off for Boston with a walk and then stole second base. On a 1-0 pitch, Eduardo Nuñez hit a ground ball to the pitcher, Scott Alexander who botched the flip to first, allowing Holt to score. Boston was ahead 2-1 and on the verge of taking a nearly insurmountable 3-0 series lead. In the bottom half of the thirteenth, Nathan Eovaldi lost the leadoff man Max Muncy on a walk. With one away, infielder Eduardo Nuñez made a wonderful play on a pop fly from Cody Bellinger. However, he fell into the stands and in doing so, allowed Muncy, the tying run, to advance to second. And then, similar to the top half of the inning, a defensive blunder allowed the run to score. Second baseman Ian Kinsler fielded a grounder off the bat of Yasiel Puig and threw the ball wide to first allowing Muncy to score. The game was tied again. Both teams traded zeroes in the fourteenth inning. In the fifteenth inning, Mookie got the chance to be one of the night's heroes. He stepped up to the plate with two outs and the go-ahead to run at second. Facing Kenta Maeda, the Dodger's seventh pitcher of the evening, he worked the count to 2-2 before taking a called third strike to end the inning, a questionable call from home plate umpire Ted Barret, causing Mookie to jump up in dismay.

Three more innings came and went. Nathan Eovaldi had pitched brilliantly in relief for Boston and was entering his seventh inning of work in the bottom of the eighteenth when Max Muncy delivered the decisive blow, taking an outside cut fastball the other way just over the fence in left. [cix]When he touched home plate, seven hours and twenty minutes had gone by since the first pitch and so too had the longest game in World Series history both by time elapsed and innings. [cx] For the Dodgers, it was an imperative win as they avoided falling into an untenable 0-3 deficit. It was also the sort of win that could swing the momentum of a series. For Mookie and the Red Sox, they were determined to put the loss past them and focus on another win.

Thus, the stage was set for Game 4 the following night with the Dodgers starter Rich Hill set to face his former club and Eduardo Rodriguez, the man on the mound for Boston. Both pitchers were on their game as they matched zeroes throughout the first five innings. In the bottom half of the sixth, the Dodgers scored first on a throwing error from catcher Christian Vázquez. With two on and two away, Yasiel Puig put a charge into the Los Angeles crowd launching a three-run shot into the seats in left. Rodriguez could only throw his glove on the mound in disgust as the Dodgers took a commanding 4-0 lead. But the Red Sox did what great teams do, they got back up. The Boston offense immediately responded in the seventh when pinch hitter Mitch Moreland connected for a three-run shot off reliever Ryan Madson. Rich Hill groaned in dismay from the dugout as the lead he had been given disappeared. Boston's Steve Pearce tied it up with a solo home run off Kenley Jansen in the top of the eighth.   In the ninth, Boston's unrelenting offense was at it again as they burst through scoring five runs, one from Mookie who was walked intentionally. The big hit in the inning came from Steve Pearce, a bases-clearing double to the gap in right center. It proved to be too big of a deficit for the Dodgers to overcome as they dropped Game 4 by a final score of 9-6 putting Mookie and the Red Sox just one win away from the Commissioner's Trophy. [cxi] For the Dodgers' Clayton Kershaw, who had lost Game 1, it was a chance for redemption. Steve Pearce greeted him rudely, launching a two-run shot into the seats in left in the first inning. Mookie was there at the top step of the dugout to greet his teammate Pearce, a longtime veteran journeyman who would hit another home run later in the game while being named the year's World Series MVP. ^{cxii} In the bottom half of the inning, the Dodgers' David Freese ambushed Boston starter David Price on the first pitch, connecting for a solo shot, trimming the deficit to 2-1. The score would stay that way until the sixth inning. Mookie, who was hitless during his last thirteen at-bats, stepped up to the plate with one away and the bases empty. Kershaw had rebounded beautifully after the Pearce home run in the first. On a 2-2 pitch, Mookie turned on it and drove it to left. Kershaw knew immediately, his knees buckling on the mound as he turned to look, only to find that it was gone. Mookie had delivered his first career postseason home run, at a critical juncture, which put the Red Sox back up by two in what would end up being the World Series clincher. Meanwhile, David Price was phenomenal in what would end up being his finest moment as a Red Sox team member. He held the Dodgers to just a single run through seven innings before leaving in the eighth. In the bottom of the ninth, with the Red Sox winning 5-1, manager Alex Cora summoned Chris Sale to close it out against the heart of the Dodgers order. He got Justin Turner swinging on a dropped third strike; catcher Vázquez threw to first. One out. Enrique Hernández followed and struck out swinging. Two out. Manny Machado stepped up to the plate and quickly fell behind in the count 1-2. The entire Red Sox team eagerly waited on the top step of the dugout, ready to explode in excitement. Sale set and delivered. Manny Machado swung and whiffed on a nasty, knee-buckling slider, [cxiii] and it was over! The Red Sox won! Sale raised his arms in triumph. Boston's catcher Christian Vázquez ran to the mound to embrace his pitcher, and Mookie made a beeline from right to meet his team on the mound.

Three days later, on Halloween, the team returned to Boston to celebrate with a parade onto Lansdowne street just outside of the old, fabled Fenway Park. Players gathered onto duckboats and cheered with the massive crowd of fans that had gathered to celebrate the team that had fought for the past six months. [cxiv]For that shining moment, Mookie and the 2018 Red Sox were at the pinnacle of the baseball world they had dominated from start to finish and had delivered for their fans a season to remember, capturing their franchise's ninth title.

Two weeks later, Mookie was announced as the American League's Most Valuable Player, putting a bow on what was a scintillating season from the 26-year-old superstar. He was Boston's first MVP since Dustin Pedroia a decade ago. And he joined an exalted group of Red Sox to win the award including Hall of Famers Tris Speaker, Jimmie Foxx, Carl Yastrzemski, Jim Rice, and, of course, Ted Williams. His 2018 season was truly one for the ages as he became the first player in Major League history to win the batting title while also recording thirty home runs and thirty stolen bases. Mookie, as always, downplayed the individual accolade acknowledging instead what his team had accomplished, saying, "It's definitely a special award and something that I cherish, but I think the most important thing is that we won a World Series and got to bring a trophy back to Boston."[cxv]

Chapter 7: The 2019 Season & a Farewell to Fenway

The 2019 season ended up being a tough one for Boston. They treaded water in the first two months, finishing May with a record of 29-28, but they had fallen a distant eight and a half games behind the division-leading Yankees. [cxvi]On June 30th, Mookie was elected to his fourth consecutive All-Star game, this time as a reserve. [cxvii]On July 26th, the Red Sox were hosting the Yankees, the second game of a four-game set. Mookie led off the bottom of the first with a bang, taking a 3-2 offering from James Paxton deep into the Monster seats in left. In his next at-bat, leading off the bottom half of the third, Mookie did it again, victimizing Paxton with a solo shot to the Monster seats in left. His next at-bat came in the bottom of the fourth. Naturally, he did it again, the only difference being that there was a runner on base. His third home run of the evening staked Boston to a 7-0 lead. [cxviii]His latest performance marked the fifth time in his career that Mookie had hit three home runs in a game, tying him with Alex Rodriguez, Mark McGwire, Dave Kingman, Carlos Delgado, and Joe Carter for the second-most in history. [cxix]

Boston's ace Chris Sale dealt with elbow issues and went on the injured list in August. An ensuing consultation with Dr. James Andrews resulted in their ace being shut down for the remainder of the year. [cxx]It was more or less the final nail in the coffin for the Red Sox 2019 season as their chances at a Wild Card berth were slim to none, the division having already been long gone. Approaching the final two weeks of the season, Mookie's slash of .293/ .391/ .527, [cxxi] while still excellent overall, paled in comparison to what he had done in the last year. But, in all fairness, it almost had to be that way, considering how special his 2018 season had been. Still, he had, for the second year in a row, led the league in runs scored. He had also continued his excellence in the field, earning his fourth-straight gold glove award while finishing seventh among all American League outfielders in defensive runs saved. [cxxii]

On September 29th, the final game of the regular season, the Red Sox were long out of contention and were hosting the Baltimore Orioles, a team that had managed to lose an astounding 107 games. It was the bottom of the ninth and the game was tied 4-4. Mookie led off the inning with a walk. Rafael Devers followed and hit a weak ground ball through the infield and into right. Mookie motored to third, then watched Orioles' right fielder Stevie Wilkerson field the grounder in right observing his seeming air of indifference. He saw his opening when Wilkerson's lackadaisical lob floated into the infield, giving him enough time to dash home and score the game's winning run, bringing the 2019 season to a close, [cxxiii] and with it, Mookie's career in Boston—but not before he had given the fans at Fenway one last moment to cheer: one final chance to adore the player that never took a single moment for granted and whose unrelenting competitive pertinacity had spurred the Red Sox to perhaps their finest season in franchise history just a year ago.

Speculation about Mookie's future in Boston had been swirling for a while now. The Red Sox had avoided arbitration with their star outfielder in the 2018 offseason, agreeing to terms on what was then a record $20 million salary for a player in their second year of arbitration eligibility. [cxxiv]In January of 2020, both sides came to terms on a one-year pact, avoiding arbitration and once again it was a record-breaking figure this time worth $27 million. [cxxv] The star outfielder had been clear in his intent to pursue free agency where he would almost certainly receive a lucrative, multi-year contract. And now that time was fast approaching, as he was on track to be a free agent following the 2020 season. The Red Sox had reportedly offered him more than one contract extension, but it became increasingly clear that the two sides were far apart financially. Mookie later described the difficulty he had in turning down an extension. It was a lot of money, the most he had ever seen. But he had to hold fast to what he believed to be a fair figure. Neither side could come to terms and at the end of the day, it was just business. cxxvi

The Red Sox then had to seek a trade partner, as they would only receive a compensatory draft pick if they were to let him walk via free agency. They had begun talks with the Dodgers and Padres, both teams made sense in that they were National League teams that had the caliber of prospects to get the deal done. Trade rumors were ubiquitous, and on February 10th, 2020 the deal was official. The Red Sox agreed to send Mookie Betts and David Price to the Los Angeles Dodgers in exchange for outfielder Alex Verdugo and prospects Jeter Downs and Connor Wong.cxxvii Alex Verdugo was a young player who had shown some promise with a .817 OPS in 2019,cxxviii but he was, of course, nowhere near the caliber of player that Mookie was. The Boston front office had cited payroll flexibility as an impetus moving forward;[cxxix] they needed to get under the luxury tax threshold and this had allowed them to do so while also acquiring a few young, cost-controlled players. For Red Sox fans it was an ignominious pill to swallow, in essence, the move was viewed as a salary dump. To lose a homegrown star who was just entering the prime of his career at 27-years-old and on his way to being a generational type of player as simply a casualty to get under budget was a bridge too far and it created a tense rift between the fans and the front office in Boston.

And so did an unforgettable chapter in Fenway Park's venerable history draw to a close; Mookie Betts was a Red Sox no more.

Chapter 8: From Boston Red to Dodger Blue & a Season Like No Other

The Dodgers were a team searching for their first World Series title in over thirty years. They had won their division every year going back to 2013 and had fallen painfully short in 2018, losing the decisive Game 7 to the Houston Astros in the Fall Classic. They were an aggressive organization that spent money and were not afraid to acquire big-named talent either on the trade market or in free agency. Manny Machado was an example, whom they acquired from the Orioles just prior to the 2018 trade deadline. And now the Dodgers believed they finally had their man. With Mookie's alluring ability now added to an already incredibly talented roster that included a three-time Cy Young award winner in Clayton Kershaw, along with the National League's 2019 MVP Cody Bellinger, the Dodgers believed they were at last poised for a championship. And they did not stop there. Just before the season was set to begin, the Dodgers announced that they had signed Mookie to a record-breaking twelve-year extension worth $365 million, just edging out Mike Trout's $360 million extension with the Angels as the biggest in baseball. cxxx

"When he talks, people listen to what he's saying", cxxxi said Dodgers' rookie second baseman Gavin Lux about his new teammate. Somewhere along the way, Mookie had made the transition to not only a remarkable baseball player but as a leader too. He was no longer that young kid who had debuted in Boston with legends like Dustin Pedroia and David Ortiz in the forefront. His reputation had now preceded him. He was in the spotlight now. His words held weight and his new team was eager to learn from him because he knew what it was like to be a part of a championship team. On February 19th, at Camelback Ranch, the Dodgers' spring training complex, Mookie took time to speak to more than 100 people in the Dodgers organization, and what he had said made an impression. There was a new feeling in the air; the Dodgers were ready to move with purpose and intention this upcoming season.

Then everything turned upside down. The COVID-19 pandemic cast a shadow of doubt across the entire world, especially the baseball season. On March 12, 2020, Major League Baseball canceled Spring Training and announced that the start of the regular season would be delayed by at least two weeks. [cxxxii]The season was then further delayed in accordance with CDC recommendations. [cxxxiii] Baseball was now, like almost everything else, officially in limbo. Then in late June, after extensive back and forth negotiations between the MLB Players Association and team owners, a plan was finally agreed upon. Players would report for Spring Training again on July 1st with Opening Day tentatively scheduled for July 23rd.[cxxxiv]

This was an extraordinary year that would bring incredible new challenges. Baseball was no different.

Gone was the comforting lull of a 162-game marathon where teams could afford to play the long game and wade through the proverbial peaks and valleys. Now, there was chaos, a sixty-game schedule would change the dynamic of how teams approached each game. Every win met that much more. In an effort to reduce travel, the schedule was limited to 40 games against divisional opponents and 20 games against teams in the same division in the opposite league. But there was more too. Double-headers were changed to seven-innings; the Designated Hitter was added in the National League along with a ghost runner in extra-inning games, and most importantly, strict social distancing guidelines and daily COVID-19 testing brought something no one had ever seen before. Players who tested positive for the COVID-19 virus were placed on a specifically designated IL (injured list) and were required to isolate themselves before needing two subsequent negative tests, taken 24 hours apart from each other before they could be eligible to return to play. All members of traveling teams were prohibited from leaving their team hotel. [cxxxv]Players, coaches, and personnel all had to be vigilant and responsible for their actions to the utmost degree in order to contain the virus while also, somehow, managing to play baseball. One false step, one indiscretion could compromise everything. The League was plagued by an uneasy feeling that everything could come crashing down at a moment's notice.

Outcries against systemic racism and social injustice came rushing to the forefront too. On Opening Day, July 23rd, there was a special ceremony initiated by the Players Alliance before all the games across the league. Players knelt along the foul lines and held a black ribbon in solidarity. The goals of the Players Alliance were to support diversity throughout baseball while standing against racial injustice and inequality. [cxxxvi] During the National Anthem, Mookie was one of the players who took a knee. He spoke about it afterward saying, "I think kneeling is definitely something that shows we need change, but also I have to put some actions into play as far as away from MLB. That's my primary goal. Today was just to unify both sides and just to show that we are here for a change." ^{cxxxvii} It was a change for Mookie who had previously stated that he would never kneel during the anthem out of deference for the military, his father having served in the Air Force. He acknowledged his change in thinking, saying, "I wasn't educated, that's my fault. I need to be educated on the situation. I know my dad served and I'll never disrespect the flag, but there's also gotta be change in the world, and kneeling has nothing to do with those who served our country."^{cxxxviii}

And so, it was with an air of apprehension that Opening Day finally arrived. The Dodgers won the first game of the season, topping the San Francisco Giants by a score of 8-1. Now with a game officially in the books, there was a sense that maybe, just maybe, Major League Baseball could manage to pull off what had seemed unthinkable only weeks ago: A season in the middle of a pandemic.

The 2020 season was remarkable. In the backdrop of the COVID-19 pandemic, there were games canceled and rescheduled, players opting out, players testing positive, and false positives as well. Outbreaks happened on the Miami Marlins and Cincinnati Reds, and yet somehow, someway, between all of it, baseball was played. And, of course, Mookie reached another milestone. On August 13th, he hit three home runs against the Padres, the sixth time he had achieved this in a single game, tying him with Johnny Mize and Sammy Sosa for the most all-time. [cxxxix]

The Dodgers ended the 2020 regular season with a record of 43-17, the best in baseball, and had cruised to their eighth straight National League West division title. [cxl] Prior to the end of the regular season, Major League Baseball announced a unique playoff format befitting what had been an equally unprecedented type of regular season. In total, sixteen teams were eligible for postseason play, eight from each league, two from each division, plus two wild cards from each league. The Wild Card game, which had previously been a win-or-go-home single contest, now was a best of three series. And the scheduling itself would be unique, as there would not be any off days during the divisional and championship series. This would greatly test each team's pitching depth during the best of seven league championship series. The best of three Wild Card Series would be held at the higher seed's home stadium. However, the two National League Divisional Series would be held at designated neutral parks: Globe Life Field in Arlington, Texas, and Minute Maid Park in Houston, with the former being the setting for the NLCS and World Series as well. [cxli]

The first seeded Dodgers were set to face the eighth seeded Milwaukee Brewers in the Wild Card best of three series. The Dodgers may have been overwhelming favorites, but knowing the way variance can affect a single game, the old adage "You can't predict baseball" being exceedingly prescient to that regard, it was imperative that Mookie and his Dodgers team not let their guard down. Simply put, anything could happen in a three-game series. A fluky play could easily turn a single game, and before they knew it, they could be fighting for their playoff lives. Unfortunately for the Brewers, their tall task of facing a juggernaut Dodgers team was made all the more unenviable when they lost Corbin Burnes to an oblique injury shortly before the series began. [cxlii] Burnes had emerged as one of the game's best young pitchers and earned consideration for this year's N.L. Cy Young Award.

The Dodgers ended up taking Game 1 by a score of 4-2. [cxliii] Dodgers ace Clayton Kershaw then got the job done in Game 2, blanking the Brewers across a masterful eight-inning performance. Mookie's two RBI double in the bottom of the fifth turned out to be all the offense they needed, generating a final score of 3-0. cxliv

For the best of five divisional round, the scene shifted to Globe Life Field in Arlington, a designated neutral field as part of Major League Baseball's health and safety provisions during the pandemic. The Dodgers were set to face their division rivals, the upstart San Diego Padres. Led by the magnetic and exceedingly talented Fernando Tatís Jr, the son of a former big leaguer, the Padres had electrified baseball fans in southern California that summer. Game 1 started off as a pitcher's duel, both teams exchanging zeroes in the run column before the Dodgers fiery, young ace Walker Buehler ceded the game's first run in the top of the fourth courtesy of a single off the bat of Padres catcher Austin Nola. The Dodgers trailing 1-0, Mookie stepped up to the plate in the bottom of the fourth inning with the bases full and two away and flew out harmlessly to left. The Dodgers later tied it up in their half of the fifth on a throwing error from second baseman Jake Cronenworth. Mookie redeemed himself in his next at-bat, ripping a double down the line in left, sending Chris Taylor to third who later scored what would end up being the winning run as the Dodgers went on to take Game 1 by a final of 5-1. [cxlv]

Game 2 got off to a similar start with the Padres drawing first blood with outfielder Wil Myers tagging Clayton Kershaw for an RBI double in the second. The Dodgers bounced right back, though, and took the lead in the bottom of the third with a two RBI double from shortstop Corey Seager. Cody Bellinger, however, ended up being the star of the game. The 2019 N.L. MVP crushed a solo home run to center field to lead off the bottom of the fourth. Later he made a phenomenal defensive play with the game in the balance. In the top of the seventh, with two outs, a runner on second, and the Dodgers holding a precarious 4-3 advantage, the young star Fernando Tatís Jr stepped up to the plate and tagged a pitch to deep center field, Bellinger drifted back, scaled the wall and brought back what would have been the go-ahead run. Mookie had a pair of singles, finishing the night 2-4 with a run scored as the Dodgers went on to win what was a spirited and closely contested game between two rivals by the final of 6-5. cxlvi

The Padres very briefly took a 2-1 lead in the bottom of the second inning, but Game 3 quickly became a rout in favor of the Dodgers with a five-run outburst in the top of the third. That rally started, of course, with a leadoff walk from Mookie. The Padres, facing elimination after losing the first two games of the series, were unable to mount any sort of a comeback and the Dodgers took Game 3 by a final score of 12-3, completing the sweep of the Padres in the Divisional round. cxlvii

The Atlanta Braves had won the National League East for the third season in a row, this time with a record of 35-25. Similar to the Dodgers, they too had needed just three games to dispatch their divisional round adversary, the Marlins. Led by an extraordinary young talent in Ronald Acuña Jr., one of the finest hitters in baseball, Freddie Freeman, and their sensational switch-hitting second baseman, Ozzie Albies, they had the star power to match the Dodgers. The stage was set for the NL pennant: a highly anticipated heavyweight fight between two of baseball's best teams.

Game 1 was a classic pitcher's duel between Atlanta's hard-throwing southpaw Max Fried and the Dodgers righty ace Walker Buehler. Atlanta struck first with a solo shot from Freddie Freeman in the first inning. The Dodgers tied things up in the fifth but then both offenses fell silent. The Braves, however, ended up victorious as their offense broke the 1-1 tie with a four-run outburst in the top of the ninth, a two-run shot from Ozzie Albies being the key hit. The Dodgers went down quietly in the ninth, with a final score of 5-1. [cxlviii]

Game 2 was an exciting contest that featured scoring on both sides. Braves' rookie Ian Anderson started the game and pitched well, but the Dodgers worked his pitch count, forcing him to leave after just four innings. Even though Mookie was not having a loud post season so far in terms of RBI or extra base hits, he continued to be a tough at-bat for opposing pitchers by refusing to expand the strike zone. It was evident as he drew two early walks off Anderson. Once again, the Braves struck first with a two-run home run off the bat of Freddie Freeman, his second of the series, in the top of the fourth. The Braves offense added four runs in the fifth to take a commanding 6-0 lead before eventually adding two more. The Dodgers offense would make it a game late, Max Muncy hitting a two-run shot in the bottom of the ninth to trim the lead to 8-6, forcing Braves' manager Brian Snitker to summon his closer, Mark Melancon. Cody Bellinger added an RBI triple to make it an 8-7 game, but the spirited comeback would fall short as the veteran closer got the job done, inducing an AJ Pollock groundout to end the game. [cxlix] When it was over, Mookie and the Dodgers found themselves staring at a precarious 0-2 series hole.

Game 3 took on must-win status for the Dodgers. History had dictated such, as the 2004 Red Sox had been the only team in Major League Baseball history to overcome an 0-3 deficit in a best of seven series. [cl] The Braves turned to the rookie pitcher Kyle Wright, who had struggled immensely during the regular season posting a 5.21 ERA through eight starts. Mookie led off the game with a ground ball to third base and knowing the importance of getting off to a quick start—this being an imperative game to win-- busted it down the line to just beat out the throw to first. He then scored the game's first run on a blistering opposite field double by the future NLCS MVP shortstop Corey Seager. [cli] That first run and early lead was critical as it took pressure off the Dodgers and immediately put stress on an inexperienced and vulnerable pitcher in Wright, in turn, precipitating one of the most epic scoring barrages in the history of Major League Baseball Postseason history. Joc Pederson and Edwin Ríos hit back-to-back home runs. Corey Seager added another RBI. Mookie drew a walk and scored for a second time in the opening inning. When the dust had finally settled, fourteen batters had come to the plate and the Dodgers had blitzed the Braves for eleven runs in the first inning, the most by any team in a single inning in the history of post season play. [clii]Game 3 was over before it began, final score 15-3. [cliii]

The Dodgers struck first in Game 4 when Edwin Ríos led the fourth with a laser into the stands off the Braves' starter: the burly, rookie right-hander Bryse Wilson. Atlanta responded in the bottom of the fourth, tying the game with a Marcell Ozuna solo home run off the Dodgers ace southpaw Clayton Kershaw. It was a well-pitched game on both sides until things unraveled in the bottom half of the sixth when an RBI double from Marcell Ozuna chased Kershaw from the game. But there was more to come. By the time the sixth inning came to a close, Mookie and the Dodgers were facing a 7-2 deficit. It was too much to overcome; the Braves exacted revenge for the previous night's shellacking and handed the Dodgers a blowout 10-2 loss. [cliv]

In Game 5, the Dodgers were now facing elimination. They had exhausted all margin for error and now needed to pull off three straight victories in order to advance. The Braves turned to their hard-throwing lefty reliever A.J. Minter to start out of necessity as a result of the condensed scheduling. Minter was outstanding and held the Dodgers off the board during his three innings. In the bottom of the third, Atlanta was already up 2-0 and threatening for more with runners on second and third and only one out. It was a critical point in the game, a hit here could score two and could end up being the knockout blow for Atlanta. Dansby Swanson swung at the first pitch from reliever

Joe Kelly and hit the ball to right, a sinking flyball that could fall in. Mookie raced in and made a spectacular shoestring catch. Ozuna, the runner at third, tagged and scored on Mookie's throw home. Or did he? A video review reversed the call; Ozuna had broken for home before the catch was made, and was out. It was a fantastic defensive double play from Mookie, which not only made the tough catch, but also kept him on his feet to make the throw home. It was a huge play that kept the Braves' lead at just 2-0. The next inning, Corey Seager led off with a blistering home run to center field off the lefty Tyler Matzek who had come in to relieve Minter. It was 2-1. The game was in reach. In the top of the sixth, Dodgers catcher Will Smith got the better of Atlanta's reliever, also named Will Smith, hitting a dramatic three-run home run to flip the game in favor of Los Angeles, 4-2. In the top of the seventh, Mookie delivered a key two-out single, scoring Chris Taylor from second, padding the lead to 5-2. He would also finish the game with a stolen base and a run scored. Corey Seager followed with a two-run shot, his second home run of the evening, pushing the lead to 7-2. Game 5 went to the Dodgers 7-3. [clv] Mookie's spectacular shoestring catch with the game in the balance had helped his team to stave off elimination. His manager, Dave Roberts, said after the game, "We've had a lot of great plays this year. But if you're talking about momentum shifts, that's the play of the year for me." [clvi] He had more magic in his glove to come.

Game 6 started with a bang when the Dodgers ambushed Atlanta starter Max Fried for three runs in the first, including yet another home run from Corey Seager, his fifth of the series, setting an NLCS record. [clvii] In the top of the second, Dodgers starter Walker Buehler got into and out of trouble stranding the bases loaded and keeping the lead intact. In the top of the fifth, Marcell Ozuna was at the plate with a runner on first and two outs, the Dodgers holding the 3-0 advantage. He drilled a hanging breaking ball to

Mookie in right field. He knew it was trouble. He raced back to the track and then to the wall, turned, and leaped, catching it, Making a sensational leaping catch on a ball that would have bounced off the top of the wall for extra bases, potentially scoring Freeman from first. But instead, the inning was over and the Dodgers still held the 3-0 lead, Buehler standing on the mound with his fist in the air in triumph. The Dodgers hung on to win by a score of 3-1. clviii

Now the stage was set for a decisive Game 7. The starters were a pair of rookies in Dustin May for the Dodgers and Ian Anderson for the Braves. May ran into trouble in the first, allowing the game's first run, an RBI single from Marcell Ozuna. Atlanta leaped out to a 2-0 lead when Dansby Swanson led off the second inning with a home run into left off Tony Gonsolin, who had come in to relieve May. The Dodgers stormed back in the bottom of the third with a two-run single from catcher Will Smith. In the next inning, the Braves took the lead back with an RBI single into center from third baseman Austin Riley. At the top of the fifth, Braves ahead 3-2 with the bases empty and one away, into the box stepped Freddie Freeman, one of the game's best hitters. He swung on the first pitch from reliever Blake Treinen and drilled a pitch to right. Dodgers fans held their collective breath as they heard the crack of the bat and saw the fly ball chase Mookie to the track. At the wall he gathered himself and leaped, catching it. His glove cleared the fence in right, robbing Freeman of a home run that would have made it 4-2 Atlanta. It was his third sensational play with the glove in as many nights and when his team needed him the most, facing the pressure of elimination. A dramatic pinch-hit home run off the bat of Enrique Hernández tied the game in the bottom of the sixth. In the bottom of the seventh, Cody Bellinger delivered what would be the winning run, sending a towering flyball to the seats in right. Game 7 came to a close with an Austin Riley flyout to center, final score 4-3. [clix] The Dodgers had done it. They had fallen behind 3-1 and reeled off three consecutive wins to advance to the World Series. And they could not have done it without Mookie. Tonight, he had delivered yet another game-saving play with his glove.

During the Fall Classic, the Dodgers were set to face the Tampa Bay Rays, a team whose phenomenal pitching had led them to their first American League East Division title since 2010. Unlike the Dodgers, the Rays were a team with a modest payroll, the third-lowest in baseball in 2020. [clx]Their roster did not feature recognizable stars; instead, they were a team with movable parts that looked to exploit advantageous matchups, platooning players regularly based on favorable lefty/righty splits. They also had one of the deepest and most effective bullpens in baseball, one they had used aggressively to get to an American-League best 40-20 record. To make it to the World Series, they had beaten the Blue Jays, Yankees, and the Astros in what ended up being a tightly contested, seven-game ALCS. Their top performer in the postseason had been the right-handed Randy Arozarena, an unheralded young batter from Cuba whom the Rays had acquired from the Cardinals this past offseason.

In the fifth inning of Game 1, with the Dodgers ahead 2-1, Mookie did what he did best: put the pressure on the opposing defense. He led off the inning with a walk and knowing that the Rays starter, six-foot-eight Tyler Glasnow, was slow to the plate, he stole second base, then he and teammate Corey Seager pulled off a double steal. With the infield drawn in, Max Muncy grounded out to first baseman Yandy Díaz who threw home, but Mookie was too quick and beat the throw sliding home to put the Dodgers ahead 3-1. The rushed throw from Diaz was a little wide of the plate allowing Seager to move to third. The Dodgers added three more runs in the inning en route to an easy 8-3 Game 1 victory but not before another Mookie milestone. Leading off in the bottom of the sixth he drove the first pitch from reliever Josh Fleming over the fence the opposite way in right, achieving his first career postseason home run with the Dodgers. clxi

In Game 2, Brandon Lowe hit a pair of opposite field home runs for the Rays. Their starter Blake Snell pitched well early, racking up nine strikeouts, but was chased in the fifth inning after a walk and a two-run home run from Chris Taylor. A Corey Seager leadoff home run in the bottom of the eighth closed the gap to 6-4, clxii but that would end up being the final as the Rays were able to hold on to tie the series up.

The Dodgers got off to an early lead thanks to Justin Turner who sent a 1-2 fastball from Rays' starter Charlie Morton over the left field wall in the first inning. Mookie had two hits, including an RBI single in the top of the fourth that staked the Dodgers to a 5-0 lead. He also added two stolen bases for good measure. The story of the game, however, was Dodgers starter Walker Buehler who piled up ten strikeouts en route to a dominating six-inning performance, allowing just a single run. The Dodgers took Game 3 by a score of 6-2. [clxiii]

For the second night in a row, Justin Turner got the scoring started with a solo home run, this time off the soft-tossing southpaw Ryan Yarbrough and putting him ahead of Hall of Famer Duke Snider for the most postseason home runs in Dodgers franchise history. [clxiv] Corey Seager hit his eighth home run of the postseason in the third, making it 2-0 Dodgers. The Rays Randy Arozarena responded in the bottom of the fourth, launching a home run to right center. The Cuban native was in the middle of a transcendent postseason performance, his ninth blast setting a Major League Baseball record for most home runs in a single postseason. [clxv] In the top of the sixth, Enrique Henández came up with two out and two on and laced a double past Rays third baseman Mike Brosseau plating Will Smith to give the Dodgers a 4-2 lead. The script flipped on a dime in the following frame with Brandon Lowe launching a dramatic three-run home run the opposite way to left off Dodgers reliever Pedro Baez, of a sudden giving the Rays held a 5-4 lead. The see-saw contest continued in the top of the seventh, this time Joc Pederson put the Dodgers back on top with a two-out, two-run single to make it 6-5 in favor of Los Angeles. The Rays responded again the next inning, this time a Kevin Kiermaier solo shot to right tied it up. And then the Dodgers took the lead again with yet another two-out hit, this time a bloop single to shallow left field courtesy of shortstop Corey Seager to give the Dodgers a 7-6 advantage. Mookie had a quiet night at the plate going 0-5, in what turned out to be a sensational win for the Rays as they took Game 4 in walkoff fashion thanks to an unbelievable error from Dodgers catcher Will Smith, Randy Arozarena slid home to score the game-winning run.[clxvi] With that 8-7 victory, the Rays had tied up the series.

Mookie led off Game 5 with a blistering double to left field and then scored on a single from Corey Seager, setting the tone early as the Dodgers looked to rebound.

Joc Pederson made it a 3-0 lead for the Dodgers with a solo home run. Then in the bottom of the third Mookie made a rare mistake, misplaying a liner to right field from Yandy Díaz, resulting in an RBI triple. Arozarena then hit a single, scoring Díaz and cutting the Dodgers lead to 3-2. It was another record, his 27th hit being the most ever in a single postseason. [clxvii] Max Muncy unloaded on a moon shot to right field off Tyler Glasnow in the top of the fifth producing the game's final score of 4-2 as Dodger pitching held tough the rest of the way. [clxviii] They were now just one win away.

October 27, 2020 marked Game 6. The Rays Blake Snell overpowered Mookie with a fastball up to end the bottom of the third, down swinging. Heading into the bottom of the sixth, the Rays held the slimmest of leads, 1-0 thanks to Randy Arozarena's tenth home run of the postseason. And then following a one-out seemingly innocuous single from Dodgers catcher Austin Barnes, Rays manager Kevin Cash made the trek out of the dugout to yank his starter Blake Snell who had allowed only two base runners so far, a pair of singles and on only 73 pitches. In stepped reliever Nick Anderson, one of the best in the league during the regular season but he had not had good results so far in the postseason. Into the box stepped Mookie. He took the first two pitches to get ahead in the count 2-0: a fastball count. Mookie swung and laced the ball fair down the line in left, racing to third was Barnes. He was now standing on second base with a double. Corey Seager stepped up and Anderson uncorked a wild pitch that slipped past catcher Mike Zunino, and Barnes scored. Just like that, the game was tied, and Mookie advanced to third. Seager then grounded out to first baseman Ji-Man Choi who threw home, but Mookie was too quick. He slid home and beat the throw. Now the Dodgers had the lead 2-1. After his home run in the bottom of the eighth off Pete Fairbanks had landed past the wall in left center, the Dodgers held a 3-1 lead and they were now just three outs away. The hard-throwing lefty Julio Urías was in for his second inning of work. Manuel Margot led off with a fly ball to deep center field, caught by Cody Bellinger. One out. Mike Brosseau stepped in to pinch hit for Joey Wendle. He went down looking on six pitches. Two outs. Urías was in attack mode and got ahead 0-2 on shortstop Willy Adames. Urías set at the belt, kicked, and fired a fastball dotting the inside corner at 97 miles per hour. The umpire called strike three, [clxix] and the Dodgers were back on top. Their World Series drought had at long last come to an end after thirty-two years. They had won it all in spite of all the challenges presented by what was quite possibly the most unforgettable season in the history of baseball. In what turned out to be the World Series clincher, Mookie had been the difference maker, scoring two of his team's three runs, one a home run, while helping to advance the other with a double.

Chapter 9: Personal Life

In January of 2021, Mookie got engaged to his girlfriend Brianna Hammonds after having been together for over fifteen years. They had first met back in Nashville as middle schoolers, and in an interview with *People* following his World Series win with the Dodgers in 2020, he shared his joy in being engaged to his longtime beloved saying, "Winning another World Series was great, but putting a ring on my MVP is the real blessing! I am a blessed man." [clxx] Together they have a daughter, Kynlee Ivory, who was born in November 2018, shortly after Mookie won the World Series as a member of the Boston Red Sox.

Mookie is an avid bowler and has been since his youth, having bowled professionally. Shortly after winning the 2018 World Series with Boston, he bowled a 300 game in the last qualifying round of the World Series of Bowling in Reno, Nevada. To that point, it was his tenth perfect game on record and first in a Professional

Bowlers Association tour event. Every year he also hosts a Christmas Bowling Tournament and Fundraiser in his native Tennessee. [clxxi]

One of Mookie's cousins is Nick Shumpert, son of former big leaguer Terry Shumpert. Nick was a former top prospect, who was selected by the Detroit Tigers' 2015 MLB draft, but turned down the offer. He was with the Braves organization briefly but was released and had been out of professional baseball since 2018. That was until Mookie saw something he liked. He was in Nashville following his World Series victory with the Dodgers in 2020 and was coaching his younger cousin when he spontaneously set an iPad atop a makeshift tripod and Facetimed two Dodgers hitting coaches so they could get a look at his cousin's swing. Shortly thereafter, the Dodgers signed Nick to a minor-league deal. [clxxii]

Mookie's intense competitiveness and concentration were cultivated at a young age. Reflecting on her son's perseverance on the field, his mother said, "When he was 10, we didn't let him win. That's why he concentrates so hard, because he does not like to get beat." clxxiii His tenacious resolve is something that has helped him not only throughout his Major League career but also early on in the minor leagues after struggling initially. His father, Willie Betts, characterized it, saying, "He's got that drive to say that it's on you to do it and I think that was one of the driving forces." clxxiv

In November of 2020, his hometown honored him with a surprise ceremony. There at Overton High School, they retired his number seven jersey. The mayor of Nashville, John Cooper, also proclaimed November 12th, 2020 as 'Mookie Betts Day' in recognition of his achievements and contributions to the community. During the COVID-19 pandemic, Mookie had donated groceries and lunches to local residents and hospital workers while also being engaged in several charities. He even assisted with batting practice at his high school, saying, "Helping people is something I enjoy doing. I like to come back here and do what I can and for the mayor to know about it definitely means I'm doing something right."[clxxv]

Chapter 10: Legacy and Future

WAR, which is short for Wins Above Replacement, is a metric that attempts to quantify a player's value in wins relative to a hypothetical replacement-level player at the same position. [clxxvi] Mookie's 2018 season WAR of 10.4 was just the 50th time since 1901 that a player had accumulated a WAR of over 10 in a single season. Considering the previous 50 seasons, that number shrinks to just twelve, including Mookie's 2018. Mookie's 2016 season was worth a WAR of eight. Over the previous 100 years, there have been only 36 players with two seasons worth eight or more WAR and 37 of those players were inducted into the Hall of Fame. Mookie was also the 11th player to record a 10 WAR season at age 25 or younger. All of those players have been inducted into the Hall of Fame, the only exception being Mike Trout. [clxxvii]

Mookie played just five full seasons with the Red Sox, but his legacy there will never be forgotten. With his

Gold Glove in 2018, he joined Dwight Evans as the only right fielder in Red Sox history to earn multiple Gold Glove awards. [clxxviii] With Boston, he hit three home runs in a single game five times, more than even the legendary Ted Williams. [clxxix] And it was with Boston in 2018 where he had one of the most remarkable seasons in baseball history, earning the Silver Slugger, MVP, Gold Glove, while also playing for the World Series-winning team. According to *BaseballReference.com*, Mookie's 2018 season ranks second in Boston franchise history in terms of WAR from a position player (Wins Above Replacement) trailing only Carl Yastrzemski's 1967 campaign in which he won the Triple Crown and Most Valuable Player. According to *FanGraphs.com*, he accumulated 37.2 WAR during his years in Boston, which pegs him at seventh place among all outfielders in Red Sox franchise history. [clxxx]

During their remarkable path through the playoffs this past year, Dodgers fans had witnessed firsthand all the ways that Mookie could affect the outcome of a game. His prowess in the field had saved their season with their backs against the wall during the NLCS against Atlanta. His speed on the basepaths constantly put pressure on the opposing defense. His discipline at the plate was exceptional as well; he never expanded the zone, even when he made an out, it was always a stressful at-bat for the opposing pitcher.

In addition, Mookie's ability to make contact is extraordinary; his career strikeout rate of 13.3%[clxxxi] being well below the league average of just over 23%[clxxxii]. And he combines that with power, hitting one out in Game 1 of the World Series and in the clincher. But there's something else to his game that sets him apart during the bright lights of October, something that would help the Dodgers in their quest for future championships. He has an almost intangible sort of baseball sixth sense: unquantifiable, but wholly perceptible. His former teammate Brock Holt summed it up well saying, "...he's so instinctive, he sees things that other guys do not normally see, and he takes advantage of them." [clxxxiii]

Mookie is also something of a perfectionist. His best friend from high school, Andrew Montgomery, knows it well. After an impressive spring training game going 2-3 with a home run and a great catch in the field, Mookie, who was a young 22-year-old player at the time, texted his friend to complain about his mistakes that day. "Mook said he had a bad game because he had a bad read on the diving catch and his last at-bat sucked." [clxxxiv] Mookie's former Boston teammate J.D. Martinez is familiar with that perfectionism as well. He refers to it as a sort of doubt; an insatiable urge to reach the pinnacle of performance. Like someone who aspires to be the greatest, he seems to have this predilection towards self-inquiry, an insatiable urge to improve, something that every champion athlete needs to reach their greatest potential. Whatever that may be for Mookie, the baseball world can simply marvel in anticipation.

There is no denying that Mookie is well on his way to chasing more titles in Los Angeles and a plaque in Cooperstown, but his greatest legacy could be as a torchbearer for the future generation of African-American players. Major League Baseball has been under scrutiny for its efforts in promoting the game among inner-city youths, specifically those in African-American communities. It has long been noted that Black representation in baseball has been far too low, with Mookie having been the only African-American player in the 2020 World Series. He expressed his support of getting Black communities involved in the game saying, "I'm doing my part, putting some programs together to get us into baseball. But I hope everyone is watching because I'm 5'9" and 170 pounds just like the majority of us. So anything is possible." clxxxv

Final Word/About the Author

I was born and raised in Norwalk, Connecticut. Growing up, I could often be found spending many nights watching basketball, soccer, and football matches with my father in the family living room. I love sports and everything that sports can embody. I believe that sports are one of the most genuine forms of competition, heart, and determination. I write my works to learn more about influential athletes in the hopes that from my writing, you the reader can walk away inspired to put in an equal if not greater amount of hard work and perseverance to pursue your goals. If you enjoyed *Mookie Betts: The Inspiring Story of One of Baseball's All-Star Right Fielders,* please leave a review! Also, you can read more of my works on *David Ortiz, Mike Trout, Bryce Harper, Jackie Robinson, Aaron Judge, Odell Beckham Jr., Bill Belichick, Serena Williams, Rafael Nadal, Roger Federer, Novak Djokovic, Richard Sherman, Andrew Luck, Rob Gronkowski, Brett Favre, Calvin Johnson,*

Drew Brees, J.J. Watt, Colin Kaepernick, Aaron Rodgers, Peyton Manning, Tom Brady, Russell Wilson, Odell Beckham Jr., Bill Belichick, Charles Barkley, Trae Young, Gregg Popovich, Pat Riley, John Wooden, Steve Kerr, Brad Stevens, Red Auerbach, Doc Rivers, Erik Spoelstra, Michael Jordan, LeBron James, Kyrie Irving, Klay Thompson, Stephen Curry, Kevin Durant, Russell Westbrook, Anthony Davis, Chris Paul, Blake Griffin, Kobe Bryant, Joakim Noah, Scottie Pippen, Carmelo Anthony, Kevin Love, Grant Hill, Tracy McGrady, Vince Carter, Patrick Ewing, Karl Malone, Tony Parker, Allen Iverson, Hakeem Olajuwon, Reggie Miller, Michael Carter-Williams, John Wall, James Harden, Tim Duncan, Steve Nash, Draymond Green, Kawhi Leonard, Dwyane Wade, Ray Allen, Pau Gasol, Dirk Nowitzki, Jimmy Butler, Paul Pierce, Manu Ginobili, Pete Maravich, Larry Bird, Kyle Lowry, Jason Kidd, David Robinson, LaMarcus Aldridge, Derrick Rose, Paul George, Kevin Garnett, Chris Paul, Marc Gasol, Yao Ming, Al Horford,

Amar'e Stoudemire, DeMar DeRozan, Isaiah Thomas, Kemba Walker, Chris Bosh, Andre Drummond, JJ Redick, DeMarcus Cousins, Wilt Chamberlain, Bradley Beal, Rudy Gobert, Aaron Gordon, Kristaps Porzingis, Nikola Vucevic, Andre Iguodala, Devin Booker, John Stockton, Jeremy Lin, Chris Paul, Pascal Siakam, Jayson Tatum, Gordon Hayward, Nikola Jokic, Bill Russell, Victor Oladipo, Luka Doncic, Ben Simmons, Shaquille O'Neal, Joel Embiid, Donovan Mitchell, Damian Lillard and *Giannis Antetokounmpo* in the Kindle Store. If you love baseball, check out my website at claytongeoffreys.com to join my exclusive list where I let you know about my latest books and give you lots of goodies.

Like what you read? Please leave a review!

I write because I love sharing the stories of influential athletes like Mookie Betts with fantastic readers like you. My readers inspire me to write more so please do not hesitate to let me know what you thought by leaving a review! If you love books on life, baseball, or productivity, check out my website at claytongeoffreys.com to join my exclusive list where I let you know about my latest books. Aside from being the first to hear about my latest releases, you can also download a free copy of *33 Life Lessons: Success Principles, Career Advice & Habits of Successful People*. See you there!

Clayton

References

[i] Jorge Castillo, "Mookie Betts' Nashville upbringing steadied by constant caring from both parents." *latimes.com*, 22 October 2020, https://www.latimes.com/sports/dodgers/story/2020-10-22/mookie-betts-nashville-upbringing-steadied-by-caring-both-parents.

[ii] Joon Lee, "The Rise of Mookie Betts." *sbnation.com, 24 April 2015, https://www.sbnation.com/mlb/2015/4/24/8470493/mookie-betts-red-sox-prospect.*

[iii] Jen McCaffrey, "The story of Mookie Betts' rise from Nashville to Boston Red Sox franchise cornerstone", *masslive.com*, 24 March 2019, https://www.masslive.com/redsox/2015/07/boston_red_sox_mookie_betts.html.

[iv] Budd Bailey, *Mookie Betts: Baseball Record-Breaker.* (New York, NY: Cavendish Square Publishing, LLC, 2019), 17.

[v] Jessica Camerato, "Childhood Accident Put Things Into Perspective for Mookie Betts." *boston.com,* 11 September 2014, https://www.boston.com/sports/boston-red-sox/2014/09/11/childhood-accident-put-things-into-perspective-for-mookie-betts/.

[vi] Joe Rexrode, "The Mookie Betts story, starring Nashville and strong parents." *tennessean.com, 18 October 2018, https://www.tennessean.com/story/sports/2018/10/12/mookie-betts-red-sox-superstar-nashville-roots-rexrode/1500780002/.*

[vii] Pedro Moura, "Inside the mind of Mookie Betts: How he channels his intense focus and drive." *theathletic.com*, 20 July 2020, https://theathletic.com/1932530/2020/07/20/inside-the-mind-of-mookie-betts-how-he-channels-his-intense-focus-and-drive/.

[viii] "Red Sox call up former Overton star Mookie Betts." *usatodayhhs.com*, 28 June 2014, https://usatodayhss.com/2014/red-sox-call-up-former-overton-star-mookie-betts.

[ix] Joon Lee, "Mookie Betts is great at every sport he's ever played." *overthemonster.com*, 30 June 2015, https://www.overthemonster.com/2015/6/30/8422417/mookie-betts-dunking-basketballs-and-being-generally-awesome.

[x] Mike Organ, "Mookie Betts bowls perfect game right after winning Gold Glove." *thetennessean.com*, 17 November 2017, https://www.tennessean.com/story/sports/2017/11/17/mookie-betts-bowls-perfect-game-right-after-winning-gold-glove-boston-red-sox-tennessee-titans/867543001/.

[xi] Joon Lee, "Mookie Betts is great at every sport he's ever played." *overthemonster.com*, 30 June 2015, https://www.overthemonster.com/2015/6/30/8422417/mookie-betts-dunking-basketballs-and-being-generally-awesome

[xii] Brian MacPherson, "There's nothing 'light' about Mookie Betts' future." *providencejournal.com*, 4 April 2015, https://www.providencejournal.com/article/20150404/NEWS/150409615.

[xiii] Joon Lee, "The Rise of Mookie Betts." *sbnation.com, 24 April 2015, https://www.sbnation.com/mlb/2015/4/24/8470493/mookie-betts-red-sox-prospect.*

[xiv] Chip Cirillo, "Overton's Mookie Betts to sign with UT in baseball." *thetennessean.com*, 10 November 2010, https://www.tennessean.com/story/highschoolsports/2010/11/12/mookie-betts-to-sign-with-ut-in-baseball/5426459/.

[xv] Joon Lee, "Mookie Betts is great at every sport he's ever played." *overthemonster.com*, 30 June 2015, https://www.overthemonster.com/2015/6/30/8422417/mookie-betts-dunking-basketballs-and-being-generally-awesome.

[xvi] Dennis Lin, "What if The Padres had drafted Mookie Betts", *theathletic.com*, 9 September 2020, https://theathletic.com/2052205/2020/09/09/what-if-the-padres-had-drafted-mookie-betts/.

[xvii] Brian MacPherson, "There's nothing 'light' about Mookie Betts' future", *providencejournal.com*, 4 April 2015, https://www.providencejournal.com/article/20150404/NEWS/150409615.

[xviii] Anthony Castrovince, "Revisiting stacked 2011 Draft 10 years later." *mlb.com*, 9 July 2021, https://www.mlb.com/news/featured/2011-mlb-draft-revisited.

[xix] Brian MacPherson, "There's nothing 'light' about Mookie Betts' Future." *providencejournal.com*, 4 April 2015,

https://www.providencejournal.com/article/20150404/NEWS/150409
615.

xx Joon Lee, "The Rise of Mookie Betts." *sbnation.com*, 24 April
2015, https://www.sbnation.com/mlb/2015/4/24/8470493/mookie-
betts-red-sox-prospect.

xxi Dennis Lin, "What if the Padres had drafted Mookie Betts."
theathletic.com, 9 September 2020,
https://theathletic.com/2052205/2020/09/09/what-if-the-padres-had-
drafted-mookie-betts/.

xxii Jen McCaffrey, "The story of Mookie Betts' rise from Nashville to
Boston Red Sox franchise cornerstone." *masslive.com*, 24 March
2019,
https://www.masslive.com/redsox/2015/07/boston_red_sox_mookie_
betts.html.

xxiii Khari Thompson, "It's a business': Mookie Betts talks Red Sox
departure, racial justice in GQ interview." *boston.com*, 16 March
2021, https://www.boston.com/sports/boston-red-
sox/2021/03/16/mookie-betts-red-sox-gq-mlb/.

xxiv Joon Lee, "The Rise of Mookie Betts." *sbnation.com*, 24 April
2015, https://www.sbnation.com/mlb/2015/4/24/8470493/mookie-
betts-red-sox-prospect.

xxv "Mookie Betts promoted to Salem." *news.soxprospects.com*, 9 July
2013, http://news.soxprospects.com/2013/07/mookie-betts-promoted-
to-salem.html.

xxvi "Red Sox announce winners of 2013 Minor League Awards."
mlb.com, 21 September 2013, https://www.mlb.com/redsox/news/red-
sox-announce-winners-of-2013-minor-league-awards/c-61316100.

xxvii "Report: Red Sox to call up Mookie Betts."
news.soxprospects.com, 28 June 2014.
http://news.soxprospects.com/2014/06/report-red-sox-to-call-up-
mookie-betts.html.

xxviii Jen McCaffrey, "The story of Mookie Betts' rise from Nashville
to Boston Red Sox franchise cornerstone", *masslive.com*, 24 March
2019,
https://www.masslive.com/redsox/2015/07/boston_red_sox_mookie_
betts.html.

xxix Cary Osborne, "Welcome to the Bigs: The story of Mookie Betts'

MLB debut." *dodgers.mlblogs.com*, 11 September 2020, https://dodgers.mlblogs.com/welcome-to-the-bigs-the-story-of-mookie-betts-mlb-debut-5089e4ec25d2.

xxx "Chicago Cubs at Boston Red Sox Box Score, July 2, 2014." *baseballreference.com*, https://www.baseball-reference.com/boxes/BOS/BOS201407020.shtml. Accessed 15 August 2021.

xxxi Craig Calcaterra, "The Red Sox call up Mookie Betts, option Jackie Bradley, Jr." *mlb.nbcsports.com*, 18 August 2014, https://mlb.nbcsports.com/2014/08/18/the-red-sox-call-up-mookie-betts-option-jackie-bradley-jr/.

xxxii Joon Lee, "The Rise of Mookie Betts", *sbnation.com*, 24 April 2015, https://www.sbnation.com/mlb/2015/4/24/8470493/mookie-betts-red-sox-prospect.

xxxiii "Red Sox Notes: Mookie Betts, Anthony Ranaudo Shine in Win Over Rays." *nesn.com*, 29 August 2014, https://nesn.com/2014/08/red-sox-notes-mookie-betts-anthony-ranaudo-shine-in-win-over-rays/.

xxxiv Ricky Doyle, "Mookie Betts To Play Second Base For Red Sox With Dustin Pedroia Out." *nesn.com*, 11 September 2014. https://nesn.com/2014/09/mookie-betts-to-play-second-base-for-red-sox-with-dustin-pedroia-out/.

xxxv "Jeter leaves with hit and 9-5 win over Red Sox." *espn.com*, 28 September 2014, https://www.espn.com/mlb/recap?gameId=340928102.

xxxvi "Mookie Betts Stats." *baseballreference.com*, https://www.baseball-reference.com/players/b/bettsmo01.shtml. Accessed 19 August 2021.

xxxvii Gordon Edes, "Hanley Ramirez, Red Sox agree." *espn.com* 24 November 2014, https://www.espn.com/boston/mlb/story/_/id/11931183/hanley-ramirez-boston-red-sox-agree.

xxxviii "Pedroia, Ramirez power Red Sox by Phillies in opener." *bangordailynews.com*, 6 April 2015, https://bangordailynews.com/2015/04/06/sports/pedroia-ramirez-power-red-sox-by-phillies-in-opener/.

xxxix Matt Snyder, "WATCH: Mookie Betts robs homer before hitting

one of his own." *cbssports.com*, 13 April 2015,
https://www.cbssports.com/mlb/news/watch-mookie-betts-robs-
homer-before-hitting-one-of-his-own/.

[xl] Jen McCaffrey, "The story of Mookie Betts' rise from Nashville to
Boston Red Sox franchise cornerstone", *masslive.com*, 24 March
2019,
https://www.masslive.com/redsox/2015/07/boston_red_sox_mookie_
betts.html.

[xli] "Betts named AL Player of the Week", *nbcsports.com*, 22 June
2015, https://www.nbcsports.com/boston/boston-red-sox/betts-
named-al-player-week.

[xlii] "2015 Boston Red Sox Schedule." *baseballreference.com*,
https://www.baseball-reference.com/teams/BOS/2015-schedule-
scores.shtml. Accessed 15 August 2021.

[xliii] Gordon Edes, "John Farrell to return as Red Sox manager in
2016." *espn.com*, 4 October 2015,
https://www.espn.com/boston/mlb/story/_/id/13805361/john-farrell-
return-boston-red-sox-manager-2016.

[xliv] "2015 Boston Red Sox Statistics." *baseballreference.com*,
https://www.baseball-reference.com/teams/BOS/2015.shtml.
Accessed 15 August 2021.

[xlv] Gordon Edes, "John Farrell to return as Red Sox manager in 2016."
espn.com, 4 October 2015,
https://www.espn.com/boston/mlb/story/_/id/13805361/john-farrell-
return-boston-red-sox-manager-2016.

[xlvi] Bob Nightengale, "Red Sox hire Dave Dombrowski; Ben
Cherington stepping down as GM." *usatoday.com*, 18 August 2015.
https://www.usatoday.com/story/sports/mlb/2015/08/18/red-sox-hire-
dave-dombrowski-president-baseball-operations-ben-cherington-
out/31959267/.

[xlvii] "Padres trade Craig Kimbrel to Red Sox in exchange for 4
prospects." *espn.com*, 13 November 2015.
https://www.espn.com/mlb/story/_/id/14124091/boston-red-sox-
acquire-craig-kimbrel-san-diego-padres

[xlviii] Quinn Roberts, "Price charms as Red Sox announce 7-year deal."
mlb.com, 4 December 2015, https://www.mlb.com/news/red-sox-sign-
david-price-to-seven-year-deal/c-158847426.

[xlix] "Boston Red Sox at Baltimore Orioles Box Score, May 31, 2016." *baseballreference.com*, https://www.baseball-reference.com/boxes/BAL/BAL201605310.shtml. Accessed 15 August 2021.

[l] "2016 Boston Red Sox Schedule." *baseballreference.com*, https://www.baseball-reference.com/teams/BOS/2016-schedule-scores.shtml. Accessed 16 August 2021.

[li] Anthony Castrovince, "All-Star rosters packed with dynamic talent." *mlb.com*, 5 July 2016, https://www.mlb.com/news/2016-mlb-all-star-game-rosters-announced-c188071682.

[lii] Cash Kruth, "Mookie tabbed as AL's top player for July." *mlb.com*, 3 August 2016, https://www.mlb.com/news/mookie-betts-wins-al-player-of-month-for-july-c193388068.

[liii] Sean Penney, "Red Sox: Mookie Betts has a historic day at the plate." *bosoxinjection.com*, 14 August 2016, https://bosoxinjection.com/2016/08/14/red-sox-mookie-betts-historic-day-plate/.

[liv] "2016 Boston Red Sox Schedule." *baseballreference.com*, https://www.baseball-reference.com/teams/BOS/2016-schedule-scores.shtml. Accessed 16 August 2021.

[lv] "Major League Team Stats "2016" Batters Dashboard: Fangraphs Baseball." *fangraphs.com*, https://www.fangraphs.com/leaders.aspx?pos=all&stats=bat&lg=all&qual=0&type=8&season=2016&month=0&season1=2016&ind=0&team=0,ts&rost=0&age=0&filter=&players=0&startdate=2016-01-01&enddate=2016-12-31&sort=5,d. Accessed 16 August 2021.

[lvi] Ben Cosman, "Yes, David Ortiz's 2016 was the greatest final season in the last 50 years." *mlb.com*, 29 September 2016, https://www.mlb.com/cut4/david-ortiz-s-2016-was-maybe-the-best-ever-c202916636.

[lvii] "2016 Boston Red Sox Statistics." *baseballreference.com*, https://www.baseball-reference.com/teams/BOS/2016.shtml. Accessed 15 August 2021.

[lviii] Ian Browne, "Betts joins elite company with 200th hit." *mlb.com*, 20 September 2016, https://www.mlb.com/news/red-sox-outfielder-mookie-betts-gets-200th-hit-c202361684.

[lix] "2016 American League Division Series (ALDS) Game 1, Red Sox

at Indians, October 6." *baseballreference.com,* https://www.baseball-reference.com/boxes/CLE/CLE201610060.shtml. Accessed 17 August 2021.

lx "2016 American League Division Series (ALDS) Game 2, Red Sox at Indians, October 7." *baseballreference.com,* https://www.baseball-reference.com/boxes/CLE/CLE201610070.shtml. Accessed 17 August 2021.

lxi "2016 American League Division Series (ALDS) Game 3, Indians at Red Sox, October 10." *baseballreference.com,* https://www.baseball-reference.com/boxes/BOS/BOS201610100.shtml. Accessed 18 August 2021.

lxii "2016 Awards Voting." *baseballreference.com,* https://www.baseball-reference.com/awards/awards_2016.shtml. Accessed 18 August 2021.

lxiii "MLB announces 2016 Gold Glove award winners", *si.com,* 8 November 2016, https://www.si.com/mlb/2016/11/09/mlb-gold-glove-award-winners-2016.

lxiv Steve Adams, "Red Sox Acquire Chris Sale In Exchange For Yoan Moncada, Michael Kopech, Two Others." *mlbtraderumors.com,* 6 December 2016, https://www.mlbtraderumors.com/2016/12/red-sox-to-acquire-chris-sale.html.

lxv "2017 Boston Red Sox Schedule." *baseballreference.com,* https://www.baseball-reference.com/teams/BOS/2017-schedule-scores.shtml. Accessed 17 August 2021.

lxvi "Mookie Betts' 8 RBIs in leadoff spot tie MLB record." *espn.com,* 2 July 2017, https://www.espn.com/mlb/story/_/id/19792483/mookie-betts-ties-mlb-record-8-rbis-red-sox-rout-blue-jays-sunday.

lxvii Dayn Perry, "2017 MLB All-Star Game: Full AL and NL rosters, starters, reserves." *cbssports.com,* https://www.cbssports.com/mlb/news/2017-mlb-all-star-game-full-al-and-nl-rosters-starters-reserves/.

lxviii "2017 Boston Red Sox Statistics." *baseballreference.com,* https://www.baseball-reference.com/teams/BOS/2017.shtml. Accessed 18 August 2021.

lxix "2017 American League Division Series (ALDS) Game 1, Red Sox at Astros, October 5." *baseballreference.com,* https://www.baseball-reference.com/boxes/HOU/HOU201710050.shtml. Accessed 18 August 2021.

lxx "2017 American League Division Series (ALDS) Game 2, Red Sox at Astros, October 6." *baseballreference.com,* https://www.baseball-reference.com/boxes/HOU/HOU201710060.shtml. Accessed 18 August 2021.

lxxi "2017 American League Division Series (ALDS) Game 3, Astros at Red Sox, October 8." *baseballreference.com*, https://www.baseball-reference.com/boxes/BOS/BOS201710080.shtml. Accessed 18 August 2021.

lxxii "2017 American League Division Series (ALDS) Game 4, Astros at Red Sox, October 9." *baseballreference.com*, https://www.baseball-reference.com/boxes/BOS/BOS201710090.shtml. Accessed 18 August 2021.

lxxiii Mike Cole, "It's (Finally) Official: Red Sox Announce J.D. Martinez's Five-Year Contract." *nesn.com*, 26 February 2018. https://nesn.com/2018/02/its-finally-official-red-sox-announce-j-d-martinezs-five-year-contract/.

lxxiv Ian Browne, "Red Sox call up top prospect Devers for 3B." *mlb.com*, 23 July 2017, https://www.mlb.com/news/red-sox-prospect-rafael-devers-called-up-c244013352.

lxxv Daniel Rapaport, "Report: Alex Cora to be Named Red Sox Manager After ALCS." *si.com*, 19 October 2017, https://www.si.com/mlb/2017/10/19/red-sox-manager-search-alex-cora.

lxxvi "Mookie Betts 2018 Batting Game Logs." *baseballreference.com*, https://www.baseball-reference.com/players/gl.fcgi?id=bettsmo01&t=b&year=2018. Accessed 18 August 2021.

lxxvii Christopher Smith, "Mookie Betts crushes three of Boston Red Sox's six homers in rout over Angels; David Price lowers ERA to 2.25." *masslive.com*, 30 January 2019, https://www.masslive.com/redsox/2018/04/mookie_betts_bashes_2_homers_d.html.

lxxviii "Kansas City Royals at Boston Red Sox Box Score, May 2, 2018." *baseballreference.com*, https://www.baseballreference.com/boxes/BOS/BOS201805020.shtml. Accessed 18 August 2018.

[lxxix] Scott Polacek, "Mookie Betts passes Ted Williams for Most 3-HR Games in Red Sox History." *bleacherreport.com*, https://bleacherreport.com/articles/2773949-mookie-betts-passes-ted-williams-for-most-3-hr-games-in-red-sox-history.

[lxxx] "2018 Boston Red Sox Schedule." *baseballreference.com*, https://www.baseball-reference.com/teams/BOS/2018-schedule-scores.shtml. Accessed 1 September 2021.

[lxxxi] Robert Falkoff, "Betts' 100th HR starts Red Sox power surge." *mlb.com*, 6 July 2018, https://www.mlb.com/news/mookie-betts-launches-100th-career-homer-c284542898.

[lxxxii] "Complete 2018 All-Star Game rosters." *mlb.com*, 8 July 2018, https://www.mlb.com/news/2018-all-star-rosters-c284894768.

[lxxxiii] "2018 Boston Red Sox Schedule." *baseballreference.com*, https://www.baseball-reference.com/teams/BOS/2018-schedule-scores.shtml. Accessed 1 September 2021.

[lxxxiv] Matt Eppers, "Red Sox's Mookie Betts hits for first cycle of MLB season and first of career." *usatoday.com*, 9 August 2018, https://www.usatoday.com/story/sports/mlb/redsox/2018/08/09/mookie-betts-red-sox-first-career-cycle/953637002/.

[lxxxv] Craig Forde, "Sox reach several milestones in G1 rout of O's." *mlb.com*, 26 September 2018, https://www.mlb.com/news/red-sox-topple-orioles-with-big-milestones-c296099292.

[lxxxvi] "Boston Red Sox Team History & Encyclopedia." *baseballreference.com*, https://www.baseball-reference.com/teams/BOS/index.shtml. Accessed 2 September 2021.

[lxxxvii] "Major League Team Stats "2018 Batters" Dashboard: Fangraphs Baseball." *fangraphs.com*, https://www.fangraphs.com/leaders.aspx?pos=all&stats=bat&lg=all&qual=0&type=8&season=2018&month=0&season1=2018&ind=0&team=0,ts&rost=&age=&filter=&players=0. Accessed 1 September 2021.

[lxxxviii] "Mookie Betts Stats." *baseballreference.com*, https://www.baseball-reference.com/players/b/bettsmo01.shtml. Accessed 19 August 2021.

[lxxxix] Craig Edwards, "Mookie Betts' Historic Season." *fangraphs.com*,

27 September 2018, https://blogs.fangraphs.com/mookie-betts-historic-season/.

xc Manny Randhawa, "The 2018 Gold Glove Award winners are…" *mlb.com*, 4 November 2018, https://www.mlb.com/news/2018-gold-glove-winners-announced-c300218006.

xci "Mookie Betts Stats." *baseballreference.com*, https://www.baseball-reference.com/players/b/bettsmo01.shtml. Accessed 19 August 2021.

xcii David Adler, "100-win history for Astros, Red Sox, Yankees." *mlb.com,* 29 September 2018, https://www.mlb.com/news/yankees-join-red-sox-astros-in-100-win-club-c296551688.

xciii "2018 American League Division Series (ALDS) Game 1, Yankees at Red Sox, October 5." *baseballreference.com*, https://www.baseball-reference.com/boxes/BOS/BOS201810050.shtml. Accessed 19 August 2021."

xciv "2018 American League Division Series (ALDS) Game 2, Yankees at Red Sox, October 6." *baseballreference.com*, https://www.baseball-reference.com/boxes/BOS/BOS201810060.shtml. Accessed 19 August 2021.

xcv "2018 American League Division Series (ALDS) Game 3, Red Sox at Yankees, October 8." *baseballreference.com*, https://www.baseball-reference.com/boxes/NYA/NYA201810080.shtml. Accessed 19 August 2021.

xcvi Jeff Passan, "ALDS Game 3: Red Sox hand Yankees worst postseason loss in team history." *sports.yahoo.com*, 8 October 2018, https://sports.yahoo.com/alds-game-3-red-sox-hand-yankees-worst-postseason-loss-team-history-032442415.html.

xcvii "2018 American League Division Series (ALDS) Game 4, Red Sox at Yankees, October 9." *baseballreference.com*, https://www.baseball-reference.com/boxes/NYA/NYA201810090.shtml. Accessed 19 August 2021."

xcviii "2018 Major League Baseball Standings." *baseballreference.com*, https://www.baseball-reference.com/leagues/majors/2018-

standings.shtml. Accessed 19 August 2021.

xcix "Alex Bregman Stats." *baseballreference.com*, https://www.baseball-reference.com/players/b/bregma101.shtml. Accessed 19 August 2021.

c "Chris Sale - Stats - Pitching | Fangraphs Baseball." *fangraphs.com*, https://www.fangraphs.com/players/chris-sale/10603/stats?position=P. Accessed 19 August 2021.

ci "2018 American League Championship Series (ALCS) Game 1, Astros at Red Sox, October 13." *baseballreference.com*, https://www.baseball-reference.com/boxes/BOS/BOS201810130.shtml. Accessed 20 August 2021.

cii "2018 American League Championship Series (ALCS) Game 2, Astros at Red Sox, October 14." *baseballreference.com*, https://www.baseball-reference.com/boxes/BOS/BOS201810140.shtml. Accessed 20 August 2021.

ciii "2018 American League Championship Series (ALCS) Game 3, Red Sox at Astros, October 16." *baseball reference.com*, https://www.baseball-reference.com/boxes/HOU/HOU201810160.shtml. Accessed 20 August 2021.

civ "2018 American League Championship Series (ALCS) Game 4, Red Sox at Astros, October 17." *baseballreference.com*, https://www.baseball-reference.com/boxes/HOU/HOU201810170.shtml. Accessed 20 August 2021.

cv "2018 American League Championship Series (ALCS) Game 5, Red Sox at Astros, October 18." *baseballreference.com*, https://www.baseball-reference.com/boxes/HOU/HOU201810180.shtml. Accessed 20 August 2021.

cvi Mike Axisa, "Dodgers vs. Rockies final score, things to know: Los Angeles wins NL West in tiebreaker game." *cbssports.com*, 1 October 2018, https://www.cbssports.com/mlb/news/dodgers-vs-rockies-final-score-things-to-know-los-angeles-wins-nl-west-in-tiebreaker-game/.

cvii "2018 World Series Game 1, Dodgers at Red Sox, October 23."

baseballreference.com, https://www.baseball-reference.com/boxes/BOS/BOS201810230.shtml. Accessed 20 August 2021.

cviii "2018 World Series Game 2, Dodgers at Red Sox, October 24." *baseballreference.com*, https://www.baseball-reference.com/boxes/BOS/BOS201810240.shtml. Accessed 20 August 2021.

cix "2018 World Series Game 3, Red Sox at Dodgers, October 26." *baseballreference.com*, https://www.baseball-reference.com/boxes/LAN/LAN201810260.shtml. Accessed 20 August 2021.

cx Scott Boeck, "Game 3 between Red Sox, Dodgers, longest in World Series history." *usatoday.com*, 27 October 2018, https://www.usatoday.com/story/sports/mlb/2018/10/27/game-3-between-red-sox-dodgers-longest-world-series-history/1786634002/.

cxi "2018 World Series Game 4, Red Sox at Dodgers, October 27." *baseballreference.com*, https://www.baseball-reference.com/boxes/LAN/LAN201810270.shtml. Accessed 20 August 2021.

cxii "Red Sox's Steve Pearce earns World Series MVP Honors." *espn.com*, 28 October 2018, https://www.espn.com/mlb/story/_/id/25113843/steve-pearce-boston-red-sox-named-2018-world-series-mvp.

cxiii "2018 World Series Game 5, Red Sox at Dodgers, October 28." *baseballreference.com*, https://www.baseball-reference.com/boxes/LAN/LAN201810280.shtml. Accessed 20 August 2021.

cxiv Whitney McIntosh, "Red Sox parade 2018: Date, time, route, and other details about the World Series celebration." *sbnation.com*, 30 October 2018, https://www.sbnation.com/mlb/2018/10/29/18036906/red-sox-parade-world-series-2018-date-time-route-closures.

cxv Richard Justice, "Betts, Yelich win first career MVP Awards." *mlb.com*, 15 November 2018, https://www.mlb.com/news/2018-bbwaa-mvp-winners-c300774262,

cxvi "2019 Boston Red Sox Schedule." *baseballreference.com*, https://www.baseball-reference.com/teams/BOS/2019-schedule-scores.shtml. Accessed 21 August 2019.

[cxvii] "2019 All-Star Game rosters announced." *mlb.com*, 30 June 2019, https://www.mlb.com/press-release/2019-all-star-game-rosters-announced.

[cxviii] "New York Yankees at Boston Red Sox Box Score, July 26, 2019." *baseballreference.com*, https://www.baseball-reference.com/boxes/BOS/BOS201907260.shtml. Accessed 21 August 2021.

[cxix] Scott Boeck, "Red Sox outfielder Mookie Betts slugs three homers in first three at-bats vs. Yankees." *usatoday.com*. 26 July 2019. https://www.usatoday.com/story/sports/mlb/redsox/2019/07/26/mookie-betts-three-home-run-yankees/1844224001/.

[cxx] Associated Press, "Red Sox shutdown Chris Sale for rest of regular season." *boston.com*, 19 August 2019, https://www.boston.com/sports/boston-red-sox/2019/08/19/chris-sale-injury/.

[cxxi] "Mookie Betts 2019 Batting Game Log." *baseballreference.com*,https://www.baseball-reference.com/players/gl.fcgi?id=bettsmo01&t=b&year=2019. Accessed 21 August 2021.

[cxxii] Paul Casella, Thomas Harrigan and Sarah Langs, "Best in field: Gold Glove Awards handed out." *mlb.com*, 3 November 2019, https://www.mlb.com/news/2019-gold-glove-winners.

[cxxiii] Pedro Moura, "Inside the mind of Mookie Betts: How he channels his intense focus and drive." *theathletic.com*, 20 July 2020. https://theathletic.com/1932530/2020/07/20/inside-the-mind-of-mookie-betts-how-he-channels-his-intense-focus-and-drive/.

[cxxiv] Katherine Acquavella, "Red Sox All-Star Mookie Betts avoids arbitration with record $20 million deal, reports say." *cbssports.com*, 11 January 2019, https://www.cbssports.com/mlb/news/red-sox-all-star-mookie-betts-avoids-arbitration-with-record-20-million-deal-reports-say/.

[cxxv] Jessica Camerato, "Mookie's arbitration deal sets record (source)." *mlb.com*, 10 January 2020, https://www.mlb.com/news/mookie-betts-sets-27-million-arbitration-record.

[cxxvi] Khari Thompson, "'It's a business': Mookie Betts talks Red Sox

departure, racial justice in GQ interview." *boston.com*, 16 March 2021, https://www.boston.com/sports/boston-red-sox/2021/03/16/mookie-betts-red-sox-gq-mlb/.

cxxvii Mike Axisa, "Mookie Betts trade: Dodgers, Red Sox finalize blockbuster after lengthy delay." 11 February 2020, *cbssports.com*, https://www.cbssports.com/mlb/news/mookie-betts-trade-dodgers-red-sox-finalize-blockbuster-after-lengthy-delay/.

cxxviii "Alex Verdugo Stats", *baseballreference.com*,https://www.baseball-reference.com/players/v/verdual01.shtml. Accessed 2 September 2020.

cxxix Eric Stephen, "Oh no, an excellent hitter returned to the Red Sox! What ever will they do?" *sbnation.com*, 5 November 2019, https://www.sbnation.com/mlb/2019/11/5/20949717/jd-martinez-contract-red-sox-mookie-betts-luxury-tax.

cxxx Jeff Passan, "Mookie Betts agrees to 12-year, $365 million extension with Dodgers." *espn.com*, 22 July 2020, https://www.espn.com/mlb/story/_/id/29517069/sources-mookie-betts-dodgers-long-term-contract.

cxxxi Pedro Moura, "Inside the mind of Mookie Betts: How he channels his intense focus and drive." *theathletic.com*, 20 July 2020, https://theathletic.com/1932530/2020/07/20/inside-the-mind-of-mookie-betts-how-he-channels-his-intense-focus-and-drive/.

cxxxii Mark Feinsand, "Opening Day delayed; Spring games canceled." *mlb.com*, 12 March 2020, https://www.mlb.com/news/mlb-2020-season-delayed.

cxxxiii Mark Feinsand, "Opening of regular season to be pushed back." *mlb.com*, 16 March 2020, https://www.mlb.com/news/opening-of-regular-season-to-be-pushed-back.

cxxxiv Ali Thanawalla, "2020 MLB Schedule: Teams to play 40 division games, 20 interleague games." *sports.yahoo.com*, 24 June 2020, https://sports.yahoo.com/2020-mlb-schedule-teams-play-052327174.html.

cxxxv Kyle Glaser, "A Guide to the 2020 MLB Season." *baseballamerica.com*, 1 July 2020, https://www.baseballamerica.com/stories/a-guide-to-the-2020-season/.

cxxxvi Eric Stephen, "Mookie Betts kneels during National anthem before first game with Dodgers." *truebluela.com*, 23 July 2020, https://www.truebluela.com/2020/7/23/21336709/mookie-betts-kneels-national-anthem-dodgers-opening-day.

cxxxvii Deyscha Smith, "Why Mookie Betts changed his stance on kneeling during the national anthem." *boston.com*, 24 July 2020, https://www.boston.com/sports/mlb/2020/07/24/mookie-betts-dodgers-kneeling-protest/.

cxxxviii Deyscha Smith, "Why Mookie Betts changed his stance on kneeling during the national anthem." *boston.com*, 24 July 2020, https://www.boston.com/sports/mlb/2020/07/24/mookie-betts-dodgers-kneeling-protest/.

cxxxix Ken Gurnick, "Mookie's sixth 3 HR game ties all-time record." *mlb.com,* 14 August 2020, https://www.mlb.com/news/mookie-betts-ties-record-with-sixth-three-homer-game.

cxl "2020 National League Standings." *baseballreference.com*, https://www.baseball-reference.com/leagues/NL/2020-standings.shtml. Accessed 24 August 2021.

cxli Anthony Castrovince, "Everything to know about expanded playoffs." *mlb.com*, 22 September 2020, https://www.mlb.com/news/mlb-announces-expanded-playoffs-for-2020.

cxlii Cliff Corcoran, "Dodgers-Brewers Wild Card Series Preview: It's a Trap!", *espn.com*, 29 September 2020, https://www.si.com/mlb/dodgers/news/dodgers-brewers-wild-card-series-preview-its-a-trap.

cxliii "2020 National League Wild Card Series (NLWC) Game 1, Brewers at Dodgers, September 30." *baseballreference.com*, https://www.baseball-reference.com/boxes/LAN/LAN202009300.shtml. Accessed 25 August 2021.

cxliv "2020 National League Wild Card Series (NLWC) Game 2, Brewers at Dodgers, October 1." *baseballreference.com*, https://www.baseball-reference.com/boxes/LAN/LAN202010010.shtml. Accessed 25 August 2021.

cxlv "2020 National League Division Series (NLDS) Game 1, Padres at

Dodgers, October 6." *baseballreference.com*, https://www.baseball-reference.com/boxes/LAN/LAN202010060.shtml. Accessed 25 August 2021.

cxlvi "2020 National League Division Series (NLDS) Game 2, Padres at Dodgers, October 7." *baseballreference.com*, https://www.baseball-reference.com/boxes/LAN/LAN202010070.shtml. Accessed 25 August 2021.

cxlvii "2020 National League Division Series (NLDS) Game 3, Dodgers at Padres, October 8." *baseballreference.com*, https://www.baseball-reference.com/boxes/SDN/SDN202010080.shtml. Accessed 25 August 2021.

cxlviii "2020 National League Championship Series (NLCS) Game 1, Braves at Dodgers, October 12." *baseballreference.com*, https://www.baseball-reference.com/boxes/LAN/LAN202010120.shtml. Accessed 27 August 2021.

cxlix "2020 National League Championship Series (NLCS) Game 2, Braves at Dodgers, October 13." *baseballreference.com*, https://www.baseball-reference.com/boxes/LAN/LAN202010130.shtml. Accessed 27 August 2021.

cl "Boston's blow out caps unequaled comeback." *espn.com*, 21 October 2004, https://www.espn.com/mlb/recap?gameId=241020110.

cli Jessica Camerato, "Seager wins MVP after record-setting NLCS." *mlb.com*, 19 October 2020, https://www.mlb.com/news/corey-seager-nlcs-mvp-2020.

clii Eric Stephen, "Dodgers set MLB postseason record with 11-run first inning." *truebluela.com*, 14 October 2020, https://www.truebluela.com/2020/10/14/21516924/dodgers-11-runs-first-inning-mlb-postseason-record-nlcs-braves.

cliii "2020 National League Championship Series (NLCS) Game 3, Dodgers at Braves, October 14." *baseballreference.com,* https://www.baseball-reference.com/boxes/ATL/ATL202010140.shtml. Accessed 28 August 2021.

cliv "2020 National League Championship Series (NLCS) Game 4,

Dodgers at Braves, October 15." *baseballreference.com*, https://www.baseball-reference.com/boxes/ATL/ATL202010150.shtml. Accessed 28 August 2021.

clv "2020 National League Championship Series (NLCS) Game 5, Dodgers at Braves, October 16." *baseballreference.com*, https://www.baseball-reference.com/boxes/ATL/ATL202010160.shtml. Accessed 28 August 2021.

clvi Anthony DiComo, "How Betts' G5 snag 'turned the momentum'" *mlb.com*, 17 October 2020, https://www.mlb.com/news/mookie-betts-makes-great-catch-marcell-ozuna-out-in-nlcs-game-5.

clvii Anthony DiComo, "Red-hot Corey Seager smashing NLCS records." *mlb.com*, 18 October 2020, https://www.mlb.com/news/corey-seager-homers-in-nlcs-game-6.

clviii "2020 National League Championship Series (NLCS) Game 6, Braves at Dodgers, October 17." *baseballreference.com*, https://www.baseball-reference.com/boxes/LAN/LAN202010170.shtml. Accessed 28 August 2021.

clix "2020 National League Championship Series (NLCS) Game 7, Braves at Dodgers, October 18." *baseballreference.com*, https://www.baseball-reference.com/boxes/LAN/LAN202010180.shtml. Accessed 28 August 2021.

clx Tyler Kepner, "World Series Preview: A Clash of Coasts and Contrasts." *nytimes.com*, 21 October 2020, https://www.nytimes.com/2020/10/19/sports/baseball/world-series-rays-dodgers.html.

clxi "2020 World Series Game 1, Rays at Dodgers, October 20." *baseballreference.com*, https://www.baseball-reference.com/boxes/LAN/LAN202010200.shtml. Accessed 29 August 2021.

clxii "2020 World Series Game 2, Rays at Dodgers, October 21." *baseballreference.com*, https://www.baseball-reference.com/boxes/LAN/LAN202010210.shtml. Accessed 29 August 2021.

clxiii "2020 World Series Game 3, Dodgers at Rays, October 23." *baseballreference.com*, https://www.baseball-reference.com/boxes/TBA/TBA202010230.shtml. Accessed 29 August 2021.

clxiv R.J. Anderson, "World Series: Dodgers' Justin Turner sets franchise record with 12th career postseason home run." *cbssports.com*, 24 October 2020, https://www.cbssports.com/mlb/news/world-series-dodgers-justin-turner-sets-franchise-record-with-12th-career-postseason-home-run/.

clxv Jesse Yomtov, "Rays' Randy Arozarena sets postseason home run record with ninth of 2020 playoffs." *usatoday.com*, 24 October 2020, https://www.usatoday.com/story/sports/mlb/2020/10/24/randy-arozarena-rays-postseason-home-run-record/6029306002/.

clxvi "2020 World Series Game 4, Dodgers at Rays, October 24." *baseballreference.com*, https://www.baseball-reference.com/boxes/TBA/TBA202010240.shtml. Accessed 31 August 2021.

clxvii Jesse Rogers, "Rays' Randy Arozarena sets record for most hits in a single postseason." *espn.com*, 25 October 2020, https://www.espn.com/mlb/story/_/id/30193479/rays-randy-arozarena-sets-record-most-hits-single-postseason.

clxviii "2020 World Series Game 5, Dodgers at Rays, October 25." *baseballreference.com*, https://www.baseball-reference.com/boxes/TBA/TBA202010250.shtml. Accessed 6 September 2021.

clxix "2020 World Series Game 6, Rays at Dodgers, October 27." *basbeballreference.com*, https://www.baseball-reference.com/boxes/LAN/LAN202010270.shtml. Accessed 6 September 2021.

clxx Conor Roche, "Mookie Betts gets engaged to girlfriend of 15 years, Brianna Hammonds." *boston.com*, 8 January 2021, https://www.boston.com/sports/mlb/2021/01/08/mookie-betts-brianna-hammonds-engaged/.

clxxi Mike Organ, "Mookie Betts bowls perfect game right after winning Gold Glove." *tennessean.com*, 17 November 2017, https://www.tennessean.com/story/sports/2017/11/17/mookie-betts-bowls-perfect-game-right-after-winning-gold-glove-boston-red-sox-tennessee-titans/867543001/.

clxxii Pedro Moura, "Dodgers sign Nick Shumpert with the help of his cousin, Mookie Betts." *theathletic.com*, 4 February 2021, https://theathletic.com/2368319/2021/02/04/dodgers-mookie-bettss-nick-shumpert/.

clxxiii Pedro Moura, "Inside the mind of Mookie Betts: How he channels his intense focus and drive." *theathletic.com*, 20 July 2020, https://theathletic.com/1932530/2020/07/20/inside-the-mind-of-mookie-betts-how-he-channels-his-intense-focus-and-drive/.

clxxiv Joon Lee, "The Rise of Mookie Betts." *sbnation.som*, 24 April 2015, https://www.sbnation.com/mlb/2015/4/24/8470493/mookie-betts-red-sox-prospect.

clxxv Mike Organ, Nashville honors MLB star Mookie Betts with his own day; Overton retires his jersey." *thetennessean.com*, 21 November 2020, https://www.tennessean.com/story/sports/columnist/mike-organ/2020/11/12/nashville-mookie-betts-day-overton-high-jersey-retired/6220046002/.

clxxvi "Wins Above Replacement (WAR)." *mlb.com*, https://www.mlb.com/glossary/advanced-stats/wins-above-replacement. Accessed 3 September 2021.

clxxvii Craig Edwards, "Mookie Betts' Historic Season." *fangraphs.com*, 27 September 2018, https://blogs.fangraphs.com/mookie-betts-historic-season/.

clxxviii Mike Organ, "Mookie Betts bowls perfect game right after winning Gold Glove." *tennessean.com*, 17 November 2017, https://www.tennessean.com/story/sports/2017/11/17/mookie-betts-bowls-perfect-game-right-after-winning-gold-glove-boston-red-sox-tennessee-titans/867543001/.

clxxix Scott Polacek, "Mookie Betts Passes Ted Williams for Most 3-HR Games in Red Sox History." *bleacherreport.com*, 2 May 2018, https://bleacherreport.com/articles/2773949-mookie-betts-passes-ted-williams-for-most-3-hr-games-in-red-sox-history.

clxxx Jake Devereaux, "All-Time Red Sox Roster: Mookie Betts." *overthemonster.com*, 29 May 2020, https://www.overthemonster.com/2020/5/29/21274147/all-time-boston-red-sox-roster-mookie-betts.

clxxxi "Mookie Betts." *fangraphs.com*, https://www.fangraphs.com/players/mookie-betts/13611/stats?position=OF. Accessed 6 September 2021.

clxxxii "Major League Total Stats "2021" Batters" Dashboard: FanGraphs Baseball." *fangraphs.com*, https://www.fangraphs.com/leaders.aspx?pos=all&stats=bat&lg=all&qual=0&type=8&season=2021&month=0&season1=2021&ind=0&team=0,ss&rost=0&age=0&filter=&players=0&startdate=&enddate=. Accessed 6 September 2021.

clxxxiii Pedro Moura, "Inside the mind of Mookie Betts: How he channels his intense focus and drive." *theathletic.com*, 20 July 2020. https://theathletic.com/1932530/2020/07/20/inside-the-mind-of-mookie-betts-how-he-channels-his-intense-focus-and-drive/.

clxxxiv Joon Lee, "The Rise of Mookie Betts." *sbnation.com*, 24 April 2015, https://www.sbnation.com/mlb/2015/4/24/8470493/mookie-betts-red-sox-prospect.

clxxxv Scott Polacek, "Mookie Betts Discusses Being the Only African American Player in World Series." *bleacherreport.com*, 21 October 2020, https://bleacherreport.com/articles/2914395-mookie-betts-discusses-being-the-only-african-american-player-in-world-series.

Made in the USA
Las Vegas, NV
09 January 2025

16113894R00085